What Readers are saying about *It's About TIME*

It's About TIME is an essential read to complete your business library. If you are looking to get more done, with less effort, in half the time, and enjoy more of what life has to offer, this resource is your solution. Full of real-life examples and strategies to inspire you to take charge of your life, this book will give you back your schedule and help you to live that life you have always dreamed of. Get ready to leverage time and regain control of destiny.

Patrick Snow
International Bestselling Author of
***Creating Your Own Destiny* and**
The Affluent Entrepreneur

Mark truly has a gift; it's understanding people. Study It's About TIME and, if you can, attend his presentations. You will be a better person for doing so. It will change your life.

Jeff Riley
Thos Somerville Co, ACCA-NCC Board

As a father, husband, contractor, and business owner, I was a motivated individual who never had enough time! Sound familiar? Mark has helped me find more time and ask different and deeper questions! He has helped me see around the corner, see the hidden, and expose a path to a better future for myself, my coworkers, and most importantly, my family! Mark Matteson Rocks!!!!!

**Joel Long, President,
Gastonia Sheet Metal, North Carolina**

Mark has done it again. Not since Freedom From Fear have I read so much useful information in such little time. This book is about more than time. It's about life and how to live it to its fullest.

**Rick Busby, Speaker,
Contractor, Author of *Simple Habits***

In his signature humble, humorous, and honest style, Mark provides us with a blueprint for a rewarding and successful life. Keep this book on your desk and study it twice a year. You'll be much better for it.

**Kevin Knebl, Speaker, Author of
*The Social Media Sales Revolution***

You uncover the causes of success in business and life. Your approach in both your writing and speaking gives us tools for change and sparks success.

—Tom Jackson, CEO, Jackson Systems

I love this book! It will be passed on to my family, friends and peers. Mark, thank you for this fantastic "how to" manual, my new daily reference tool for setting my goals, reviewing my priorities, and managing my time. All of your books have been invaluable to me, but this one has a special place on my desk, in my briefcase, on my bedside table, and on my gifts list!

**—Nancy Jones, CAE, Executive Director,
Plumbing-Heating-Cooling Contractors of Texas**

Mark clears all the smoke and mirrors and delivers a combination that results in countless productivity-enabling strategies along with the motivation and inspiration to spark action. I need a silver platter so I can properly serve up this amazing book to my family and closest friends!

**—John Bridge, President, StickyMan,
Self-Help That Sticks!**

I found this book to be easy reading, extremely informative, providing step-by-step processes, and offering powerful tools in mastering the principles that are needed to change habits and live a grateful, fulfilled life. Time IS a Gift!

—Donna Dubicki, Property Manager

I always enjoy hearing you speak and reading your tweets, monthly e-newsletters, articles, e-books, and books. They are filled with useful, life-changing information that makes a difference in both my personal and professional life.

—Kate Kelly, Editor, Penton Media

It's About TIME is an easy book to read, understand, and apply to your life right now. It's filled with tried and true advice and formulas that help you identify and isolate life challenges, implement change, and realize remarkable improvements in your life. The definition of insanity is doing the same thing over and over and expecting different results; use this book as a practical guide to change your mind and change any area of your life for the better!

Dexter Wellington, HomeStreet Bank Branch Manager/Mortgage Banker

Your writing has changed my life in a very short time. I read the books you suggest. Thank you.

—Bill McKinley, Mortgage Broker

IT'S ABOUT TIME

IT'S ABOUT TIME

TIME

How to Get Twice as Much Done
in Half the Time
and Enjoy Balance and Peace of Mind!

Mark Matteson

Published by
Tremendous Life Books
118 West Allen Street
Mechanicsburg, PA 17055
www.TremendousLifeBooks.com

Editing: Tyler Tichelaar, PhD.

Cover and Interior Book Design: Karen Webb

ISBN 13: 978-1-936354-43-6

CONTENTS

INTRODUCTION

Are you ready to embrace new and better ways of getting things done? Now is the time; today is the day for exciting and new actions. My sincere hope is that this book will inspire you, empower you, and that you will use the tools and simple strategies contained here toward improving your personal effectiveness. Others are watching you, waiting to see what you will do. Results are the name of the game. This book will assist you in achieving twice as much in half the time IF you persist in taking action every day to create a more effective YOU. In time, others will want to know how you get so much done.

Then—and only then—will you be ready to make a difference in the world by sharing it with others. Thank you for your trust. I promise you when you put this book down, you will be a different person.

Mark Matteson

1

INSPIRATIONAL DISSATISFACTION!

Have you ever heard someone say, *It's About TIME?* When things get bad enough in our lives, we are motivated to change. I like to call it INSPIRATIONAL DISSATISFACTION! This little book is something I HAD to write. These are lessons I needed to learn and then relearn. In sharing them with you, I am reminding myself that IF I practice what I preach on these pages, I will get the results I seek in a fraction of the time and effort expended. First-person experience has proven this truth time and time again. If, like me, you have ever spent an extended period of time disorganized, frantic, going 200 mph, and ultimately not getting the critical things done, you will appreciate what these simple (but not easy) ideas can do for your life. You will experience joy, balance, peace of mind, and a sense of control and effectiveness that is truly life altering. Once you have mastered some of these principles, teach them to two people you care about. You will help your friends and it will cement your learning so you can attain mastery of your time and talent. It's called "dual-plane learning."

Think of this book as a buffet. On your first visit, take a few things and put them on your plate. Taste them. How are they? Do you want seconds? On your next trip through the line, try something else. Taste it. Good huh? Have some more. Life is like that: trial and error. It's also governed by the greatest law in the universe, the Law of Cause and Effect. We reap what we sow.

Okay, let's get started....

What is time? *The American Heritage Dictionary* defines it as *a non-spatial continuum in which events occur in apparently irreversible succession*—not a very helpful definition. One mentor of mine called it event control. I prefer Ben Franklin's simple description: *Time is the stuff of which life is made.*

In my mind, the saddest phrase in the English language is *IF ONLY I HAD...* It's the pain of regret. It's not being true to yourself, your goals, objectives, and the reason you are here on earth. It's living life with sadness and beating yourself up because of past sins of omission and commission. Blame and regret, regret and blame. It's Marlon Brando in the 1954 Best Picture, *On the Waterfront:*

> *"I coulda had class. I coulda been a contender. I coulda been somebody instead of a bum, which is what I am. "*

This book is about living your life with no regrets. It is about eliminating the *IF ONLY I HAD's* in your life. If you follow the suggestions, you will live a full and rich life and accomplish twice as much in half the time. You will have realized that vast potential within you.

We have all the time there is. No one has any more or less of it: 24 hours in a day, 1,440 minutes, 86,400 seconds. Ever hear someone say, *Do you have a second?* That usually means an hour. Why don't we say no? The truth is we don't manage time very well. We are not mindful. We manage activities in relation to the sands of time, dropping through our own personal hourglass.

No time? That's a myth. Here are some other myths about time. See whether you are guilty of using one or more of these excuses. I know I am.

I am waiting until I have more time.

It (planning) doesn't work for me.

I always lose my list.

I already took a time-management course (or read the book).

You just can't get organized around here.

But there is nothing I can do.

People keep interrupting me.

Time Management is boring.

Isn't there a danger you will get so organized you can't get anything done?

I need someone to motivate me.

Is it time to be honest? Are you operating on a small fraction of your potential? Would you like to learn how to get twice as much done in half the time? If you answered yes, read on.

My mother passed away two years ago. Her sand was all gone. She was one of the best time managers I ever knew. We finally sold her house. As we divided up her lifetime of possessions, I was struck by how incredibly organized she was in every aspect of her life: finances, closets, bookshelves, scrapbooks, and pictures, even her kitchen. She labeled everything! It was clear much of what she owned reflected how proud she was of her history, British history, family history, the things she loved and cared about. Her home was a shrine to a life well lived and traveled. Some of those treasured belongings ended up in my house. Now I had nine pounds of coffee in a five-pound can. What to do? I had INSPIRATIONAL DISSATISFACTION.

I sat down and mind-mapped this massive project. I decided to go through every room, closet, nook, cranny, and shelf to purge, sort, toss, and clean. In reorganizing my bookshelf, I created a shelf just for books on time management and organization. I went back and reread the top twenty-five classics on the subject. It was a reminder of the things I used to do, but got out of the habit of doing. Good habits are hard to form, but easy to live with.

Here is my list of the very best books on the subject of effective time management. They are classics.

- *The Autobiography of Benjamin Franklin*
- *The Effective Executive* by Peter Drucker
- *How to Get Control of Your Time and Your Life* by Alan Lakein
- *Getting Things Done* by Edwin Bliss
- *How to Put More Time in Your Life* by Dru Scott
- *The Organized Executive* by Stefanie Winston
- *Time Management: An Introduction to the Franklin System* by Richard I. Winwood
- *One Thing At a Time: 100 Simple Ways to Live Clutter-Free Every Day* by Cindy Glovinsky
- *Getting Things Done: The Art of Stress Free Productivity* by David Allen
- *Benjamin Franklin: An American Life* by Walter Isaacson
- *1,000 Places to See Before You Die* by Patricia Schultz

Now, let's begin raising your personal awareness by taking a simple quiz. Be as honest as you can. No one else will see the answers but you. Simply answer YES or NO to the left of each question:

___ 1. Do I have, in writing, a clear list of Lifetime Goals?

___ 2. Do I have a similar short-term set of goals for the next six months?

___ 3. Have I done something today to move me closer to my lifetime goals or my short-term goals?

___ 4. Do I have a clear idea of what to accomplish at work during the coming week?

___ 5. Do I try to do the most important tasks during my prime time, the time of day when I am at my best?

___ 6. Do I concentrate on objectives instead of procedures, judging myself by accomplishments/results instead of activity?

___ 7. Do I set priorities according to importance rather than urgency?

___ 8. Do I make constructive use of my commute time?

___ 9. Do I delegate as much work as possible to competent associates?

___ 10. Do I delegate challenging projects as well as routine ones?

___ 11. Do I delegate authority along with responsibility?

___ 12. Do I prevent subordinates from delegating upward those decisions that they find difficult or worrisome? (Am I approachable?)

___ 13. Do I effectively leverage the time and talent of direct reports to get better control of my time?

___ 14. Have I taken steps to prevent unneeded information and publications from reaching my desk and intruding upon my time?

___ 15. When debating whether or not to file something, do I practice "If in doubt, throw it out"?

___ 15. In meetings, do I paraphrase what the issues are and summarize the decisions made and responsibilities assigned?

___ 17. Do I check my e-mail only twice a day?

___ 18. Do I put work out of my mind when away from the office, except in clear emergencies?

___ 19. Do I force myself to make minor decisions quickly?

___ 20. Am I on guard against the reactive, recurring crisis and taking measures to prevent its recurrence?

___ 21. Do I always set deadlines for myself and others?

___ 22. Do I force myself to make the time to plan daily?

___ 23. Have I discontinued any unprofitable routines, habits, or activities?

___ 24. Do I keep important things on me (my phone/briefcase) that I can work on in my spare time (waiting in line, planes, dentist's office)?

___ 25. Do I live in the present, thinking in terms of what needs to be done now instead of rehashing mistakes or worrying about the future?

___ 26. Do I make periodic use of a Time Log to determine whether I am slipping back into old, bad habits or unproductive routines?

___ 27. Do I keep in mind the dollar value of my time, the opportunity costs of ineffective habits and time-wasting pursuits?

___ 28. Do I apply the Pareto Principle (80 percent of the results come from 20 percent of the activity) whenever I am confronted with a number of tasks that need to be done?

___ 29. Am I really in control of my time? Are my actions and decisions determined primarily by me, not by external circumstances or by other people?

___ 30. Do I ask myself throughout the day, "What is the very best use of my time, right now?"

___ 31. Am I continually striving to establish good habits that will make me more effective?

Give yourself this quiz every six months. If any of the answers are NO, review those items and determine what you can do to correct the behavior. Set goals around that challenge. The price of effective time use far outweighs old, ineffective habits. Eternal vigilance is its own reward. You will get twice as much done in half the time.

To get the most from this information as you go through it, remember R2A2:

R = Recognize the principle.

R = Relate it to your world and work.

A = Assimilate the information: "Repetition is the mother of skill."

A = Apply the principle as soon as possible.

Monitor your results. Ask yourself two simple questions: What went well that I need to repeat? What can I do better next time?

Now, let's get to work on making a more effective you.

Invest a few minutes right now to capture ideas that bubbled to the surface. Write them down. In fact, read this book with a pen in hand to highlight, underline, and employ symbols like *, !, ?, and + next to passages that mean something to you.

YOUR NOTES

_____

_____

_____

_____

_____

_____

_____

_____

_____

_____

_____

_____

_____

_____

_____

_____

_____

_____

_____

2

ON HABIT AND COMFORT ZONES

In my seminars and keynotes, I have the audience fold their arms. *Which arm is on top?* I ask. Why? The simple answer is, comfort and habit. It's a comfort zone. I then have them fold their arms again with the other arm on top. "How does that feel?" I ask. "Uncomfortable!" "Awkward!" "I don't like it!" are what I hear most often. Most of the things we do are based on habit and comfort zone. Habit is second nature. Some experts say habit is ten times nature.

William James, the father of American psychology, wrote:

The more details of our daily life we can hand over to the effortless custody of habit, the more our higher powers of mind will be set free for their proper work. In the acquisition of a new (and positive) habit, there are four great maxims to remember:

1. *We must take care to launch ourselves with as strong an initiative as possible. Take a public pledge, reinforce the right motives, make engagements incompatible with the old ways.*

2. *Never suffer an exception to occur till the new habit is securely rooted in your life. Each lapse is like letting fall a ball of string which one is carefully winding up; a single slip undoes more than a great many turns will wind up again. Success at the outset is imperative. Failure is apt to dampen the energy of future attempts, whereas past successes nerve one to future vigor. Abrupt acquisition of the new habit is the best way if there be a real possibility of carrying it out. It is surprising how soon a desire will die if it be never fed.*

3. *Seize the first possibility to act on every resolution you make. With good intentions the proverbial road to hell is truly paved. A tendency to ACT becomes effectively ingrained in us only in proportion to the frequency with which the actions actually occur, and the brain grows to their use. Never should we suffer ourselves to have an emotion at reading a book without expressing it afterward in some active way.*

4. *Keep the faculty of effort alive in you by a little gratuitous exercise every day. In other words, do every day something for no other reason than you would <u>rather not do it</u>, so that when the hour of dire need draws nigh it may find you nerved and trained to the stand the test.*

If we realize the extent to which we are mere walking bundles of habits, we would give more heed to their formation. We are spinning our own fates, good or evil, and never to be undone. Every smallest stroke of virtue or vice leaves its never so little scar. If he keeps faithfully busy each hour of the working day, he may safely leave the final result to itself. He can with perfect certainty count on waking up some fine morning, to find himself one of the competent ones of his generation, in whatever pursuit he may have singled out.

Dorothea Brande, in her classic 1936 bestselling book *Wake Up and Live*, said it very simply: *Act as if it were impossible to fail.*

Everything I want is just outside my comfort zone. What got me HERE, won't take me THERE! If I practice stretching my comfort zones in the little things, when the need arises to do so in big things, I will be prepared and not feel so overwhelmed.

Here are some comfort zone-stretching exercises to prepare you for bigger changes. They work.

1. For one day, say YES to every request that comes along. In doing so, it will become apparent how

often we do things we don't want to do from fear of hurting someone's feelings.

2. For one day, say NO to every request that comes along. In doing so, you free up the necessary time to complete the things you deem important in your life and work.

3. Invest an hour one day in complete silence. Remember the acronym W.A.I.T.—"Why Am I Talking?" As I began to practice this, a tremendous feeling of worth and confidence arose in me. I realized how much time I wasted in idle chatter. As time goes by, increase it to two hours, four hours, and finally all day. Silence is golden. Great ideas will flow forth from your subconscious.

4. Learn to THINK on one subject exclusively for thirty minutes. Write out the topic in your journal at the top of the page and wait. If your mind wanders, and it will, bring it back to the subject at hand. Concentration is a muscle that grows with use.

5. Plan a two-hour period in your day down to fifteen-minute increments. Read the paper, plan your day, read a book, read your mail. Set a timer. Be ruthless with yourself. Once you are convinced of its efficacy, do it for an entire day. You will realize, as I did, how much time you waste on unimportant tasks.

6. Write an e-mail to a friend or client without using the words *I, Me,* or *Mine.* When you are forced to use the pronoun *YOU,* you will realize how much of your conversation is self-centered.

7. Keep an acquaintance or friend talking for thirty minutes without making him aware he is doing all the talking. Ask open-ended questions (WHO, WHAT, WHERE, WHEN, WHY, HOW) and listen actively. People love to talk about themselves. Moreover, you will learn so much.

8. Write a positive e-mail to a friend, relative, or client stating the Five Things You Admire about Him or Her. It will strengthen the bond between you, force you to think about his assets, and absolutely astonish him.

9. Smile at every person you meet for one day: a really big smile, heartfelt, sincere, and positive. It takes thirteen facial muscles to smile, but forty-seven to frown. Evidently some people don't mind the extra work.

10. Throw yourself out of your comfort zone with any or all of the following disciplines:

    a) Drive a different way home one day.

    b) Eat one meal with your left hand if you're right-handed (or vice-versa).

c) Read a magazine you have never read before.

d) Eat at a new restaurant, preferably one offering a foreign cuisine you have never tried.

e) Let the waiter order for you.

f) Stay up all night and work.

g) Say nothing all day except in response to direct questions. When you do answer, do it with brevity, but with a positive tone and a smile.

h) Let your wife choose the movie or have the remote control (Fellas, I can hear you groaning! "No, we will end up watching some *Eat, Pray, Love* kind of movie." Yes...and? This activity has done more to improve my marriage than almost any other idea in thirty-two years!)

First, we form habits, and then they form us. Good habits are hard to form and easy to live with; bad habits are easy to form and hard to live with. Get in the habit of stretching your comfort zones. It will change your life for the better. A wild adventure awaits.

3

LET'S ROLL UP OUR SLEEVES

Have you ever been to a buffet and been a little overwhelmed by the sea of choices in front of you? What do we do? We take a little bit here and there and try them. Content with our choice, we go back for seconds. This chapter is a different kind of buffet: food for thought, food for action, food for your consideration. Grab a big plate. Let's eat.

Here are the "Fifty-Five Great Effectiveness Ideas" from my research, my clients' successful habits, from my own experience, and oh yes, thanks Mum.

1) **Put your lifetime goal list in writing:** the 101 things you want to DO, HAVE, SEE, BECOME, and SHARE before you kick the bucket. Mine took about 45 minutes the second time. I did my first one in 1992. When I reviewed it, I realized I had accomplished about half of them.

2) **Label the Goals**: One-Year, Five-Year, Ten-Year, and Twenty-Year Goals on the left of each one.

3) **Rewrite** Your Top Ten One-Year Goals and **Prioritize** Your List 1-10.

4) **Rewrite Your Number One Goal on a 3 x 5 Card**, as if it were already true, in Goal-Achievement language: Personal, Positive, Powerful, and Present Tense (*I AM a ruthless manager of my time—Organized, Disciplined, Effective!*) along with 5-25 reasons WHY you want that goal.

5) **Bombard Your Subconscious with that One Goal.** Choose one modality that fits you. All that is needed to change your self-image (your internal thermostat regulator) is the formula I x E x R = N/R: Impression x Emotion x Repetition = New Reality! It's a daily discipline: **Write** it out in your journal, **Say** it aloud, **Visualize** it happening, or **Record** it and play it as you walk or work out at least 2-3 times a day for 90 days. Slowly, the setting on your thermostat and your corresponding comfort zone will change, as will your attitudes, behaviors,

and habits. People, opportunity, books, and ideas will come flowing into your subconscious in the form of hunches. Pay attention. Write them down as they appear. Act on them.

6) **Invest in Your Own Hour of Power.** This one daily discipline might make you the most effective person you know! The first 20 minutes invest in **Reviewing** your Number One Goal, 20 Minutes **Planning** your day, listing the Six Most Important Action Items for the Day, and 20 minutes **Reading** a book in alignment with that one goal.

7) **List Your Top Priority Actions as an "A"**: A-1, A-2, A-3, A-4, A-5, A-6; B-1, B-2, B-3, and so on. Focus on A Items first. Resist the temptation to do a B or C Item. Stay focused on what is most important to you. Most days I rarely get more than six or seven action items completed. Unfinished tasks get transferred to the next day.

8) **Become a Great Mental Manager.** Adopt this attitude and belief: *I avoid feeling guilty about what I don't do.*

9) **Say It Aloud Until It Becomes a Habit**: *I enjoy whatever I am doing. I love life!*

10) **Ask Yourself the Alan Lakein Question Throughout the Day**: *What is the best use of my time right now?*

11) **Embrace the Philosophy**: *I am a perennial optimist, grateful for what I have. I have developed a positive expectation of success in my work and at home.*

12) **Borrow Peter Drucker's Discipline**: *I do first things first, one thing at a time, and finish what I start!* That is profoundly simple and simply profound.

13) **Smile as You Say**: *I build on my success. My confidence and performance increases with each one.*

14) **Listen to Earl Nightingale's Advice**: *I avoid wasting time with regret, envy, worry, and resentment. I replace those negative emotions with the thoughts and feelings about my #1 Goal.*

15) **Memorize this Quote from Richard I. Winwood**: *I remind myself THERE IS PLENTY OF TIME FOR THE IMPORTANT THINGS. If it's important, I make time for it.*

16) **The Answer isn't More Hours**. Instead, affirm: *I work smarter, not harder. I plan my work and work my plan.*

17) **Give Yourself a Reward**. When you tackle a particularly difficult or unpleasant project and complete it, take time off for a mini-vacation, a movie, a good book, a new outfit, etc.

18) **Give Yourself an Extra Hour or Two Each Day**. Get up at 5 AM every morning (I can hear the groans). Did you know, as you get older,

most people only need six hours of sleep a night? Ben Franklin wrote, *Early to bed, early to rise, makes a man healthy, wealthy and wise.* He is right. Okay, for some of you, it means staying up an hour later at night. Og Mandino wrote his best-selling books from 10:00 PM to 2:00 AM.

19) **Skim Books Before Choosing to Read Them.** With non-fiction, read the back cover, table of contents, the first and the last paragraph of each chapter before committing to read it. NOT reading the wrong book can save you time and stress.

20) **Limit Your Television Time to Five to Seven Hours a Week.** I cancelled cable at our home in Edmonds and don't I miss it! In most U.S. households, the television is on 40 to 50 hours a week! Moderation is the key.

21) **Take a Break from the BAD News.** Avoid reading the newspaper, watching television newscasts, or listening to news on the radio. Instead, listen to educational CDs or MP3s when you drive. "Windshield University" will earn you two or three degrees in your lifetime. Commute time can be learning time; OR take this time to affirm your goals and think. I get some of my best ideas when I am driving to Lake Chelan, three hours east of my home.

22) **Walk or Ride a Bike to Work**. If that's not possible, see if you can work from home a couple of days a week. You never know until you ask.

23) **Examine OLD Habits for Possible Elimination**. What do you need to STOP doing? Bad habits are easy to form, but hard to live with.

24) **Examine and Embrace NEW Habits and Stretch Your Comfort Zones**. What do you need to START doing? Good habits are hard to form, but easy to live with.

25) **Carry a Small Journal or 3 x 5 Cards with You to Jot Down Ideas**. Okay, so that's old school. What about downloading an app for that purpose to your phone? It's the discipline that matters. When a good idea interrupts you, capture it. Do not leave it to memory.

26) **Set Your Watch or Phone 10 Minutes Fast**. This will prevent you from being late. All the clocks in my home are 10 minutes fast.

27) **Review and Revise Your "Lifetime Goals" List Once a Month**. Have you made any progress? What can you do to move toward one of them? Rick Steves, the famous travel expert on PBS, has his offices in Edmonds, Washington. I read his books before I travel internationally. Doing so saves me time and dramatically enhances the value of the trip. He conducts travel seminars and coaching sessions. Go visit

your travel agent and talk about that trip YOU would like to take.

28) **Are You AM or PM?** Are you a morning person? Plan your day in the morning. Are you an evening person? Plan your day before you go to bed each night. Each of us has a different circadian rhythm. Get in touch with yours.

29) **Surround Yourself with Reminders of Your #1 Goal**. Place signs—pictures, images, word descriptions—around your home and office that remind you of your most important goal. Put them where you will see them many times a day: car dashboard, bathroom mirror, fridge, in place of a bookmark, in your journal, in your wallet or purse.

30) **Choose a Good Calendar and Commit to Using it Every Day**. I have grown fond of my iCalendar. Like a good virtual assistant, it sends reminders to my phone! Plan your day, week, month, quarter regularly.

31) **Ask Yourself**: Would anything terrible happen if I didn't do this item? If the answer is no, don't do it. No guilt. Guilt is for people who don't know better.

32) **Say to Yourself**: *I have confidence in my judgment of priorities and stick to them in spite of difficulties.*

33) **Learn to Concentrate on One Thing at a Time**. Make mini-lists and stick to them. By the way, no flying pieces of paper allowed;

get a journal, a day planner, or use your smart phone or tablet. I love the journal function on my iPad. It's great for notes, ideas, and action items. Find what works for you and stick with it.

34) **Bundle Errands for the Non-Prime-Time Part of Your Day**. Do them in the late afternoon or evening. I frequent companies that stay open late, like Kinko's and Starbucks.

35) **Chunk Similar Action Items in One Prime-Time Sitting**. I write all three proposals I conceptually closed earlier in the day in one sitting, save the documents, and go for a walk. When I return, I edit all three in one sitting, print, double-check, and send them off. Chunking similar activities is a more effective use of your time and talent!

36) **Use the 80/20 Rule (Pareto's Law)**. Eighty percent of the results come from 20 percent of the items on your list. Eighty percent of your sales come from 20 percent of your prospects. Learn how to leverage this law.

37) **Train Yourself**: Go down your list of things to do without skipping to the easier or faster-accomplished items. Stick with the "A's" on your list until they are completed.

38) **Think of Big Projects as "Eating an Elephant"**: How do you eat an elephant? Slice it up and eat it a bite at a time. More on that later.

39) **Try the "Swiss Cheese" Method**. Sometimes starting a BIG project is hard, so shoot holes in it. Write all the things you will need to do. Review the list and do SOMETHING. At times, just starting the project by doing something will overcome your inertia and get the ball rolling. Momentum creates more momentum. Success breeds success.

40) **Focus on the Items with the Best Long-Term Benefits**. Choosing one of your long-term goals, pick one action item and do it for 15 to 20 minutes a day for 90 days. Elephant leftovers always taste better.

41) **Do Your Thinking on Paper First**. Create a mind map: write the project or goal in the center of the page and circle it. Think of it as the sun in your solar system. Add the planets *Who, What, Where, When, How,* and *Why.* Go over the planets and list the moons. Go over them again and write the number "1" next to the most important item. Number the next planet and so on until they are all prioritized.

42) **Rewrite Your Solar System List**. On a separate piece of paper, estimate how long each item will take, then get started on your #1 item.

43) **Set Deadlines for Yourself and Others**. Some of us work best with dates and timelines. Are you one of those people?

44) **Tell a Friend, Relative, or Peer About Your Goals and Deadlines.** Have him hold you accountable for their completion. Do the same for him. Talk to him at least once a month. Compare notes and progress.

45) **Work in Solitude in the Morning and Save the Afternoon for Meetings with Others.** Get the most important things done in the first part of your day. Think of it as eating your vegetables first, and then enjoy your meat and potatoes. Reward yourself with dessert.

46) **Learn to Listen Actively in Every Conversation.** Take good notes. Paraphrase what you hear to make sure you understand it. It will save you a lot of time and build the relationship at the same time.

47) **Be Mindful of not Wasting Other People's Time.** Develop empathy, respect, and compassion for friends, clients, peers, and friends. Learn to read body language; it's 55 percent of the message from others. Trust me, they will notice.

48) **Delegate, Delegate, Delegate Whatever and Whenever You Can.** Soar with your strengths and find competent people to whom to outsource your areas of weakness. Pay them well and treat them even better. Tell them what you want and why. Leave the "how" up to them.

49) **Have a Place for Everything and Everything in its Place.** (Thanks, Mum, for the able example.)

50) **Have Only ONE THING on Your Desk at a Time.** It's your A-1 Action Item. File everything else. This is huge. Clutter is a distraction.

51) **Invest the Time to Organize**: your desk, files, shelves, PC/Mac, books, cabinets, car trunk. Do it for how it will make you feel. It will build your self-esteem, self-worth, and self-respect.

52) **Enlist Help**: If you don't know how or can't bring yourself to do #51, hire someone to help you get organized, or read a book or attend a seminar. It will change your life.

53) **Adopt the 60-Second Rule**: Be able to find a document, file, book, or report in 60 seconds. If you can't, see #51 and #52! I know, I repeated this one, but it's vital. It's a "20-percenter"!

54) **If Possible, Check E-mail Twice a Day, Morning and Evening.** Napoleon responded to mail every three weeks. Resist the urge to pick up your smart phone every 10 minutes. I still struggle with this one.

55) **Go Over This List Once a Month for a Year.** Evaluate your progress and reward your new, positive *effectiveness* habits. Keep asking yourself, *Is what I am doing right now the best use of my time?*

Send this book to someone you care about, but only if he is serious about getting twice as much done in half the time. He will thank you. Send me an e-mail and tell me how these ideas are working for you. If you have some ideas for me, I will add them to the second printing with attribution. Send them to me at Mark@SparkingSuccess.net.

Time is a gift. Greet this day with eager delight as if someone who loves you gave you an unexpected gift to be embraced, savored, and enjoyed. Treat it with care. Give yourself the gift of time. You don't have to go 200 mph, frantic and stressed. You can work smarter, not harder. Life is good in the right lane going 60 mph with no stress. You have all the time there is. After all, ISN'T IT ABOUT TIME?

Full yet? That list represents some of the absolute best food for thought you will ever find on personal and professional effectiveness. Let me get you some coffee.

YOUR NOTES

_____

_____

_____

_____

_____

_____

_____

_____

_____

_____

_____

_____

_____

_____

_____

_____

_____

_____

_____

_____

_____

_____

End the day by putting it away!
— Mark Matteson

A place for everything and everything in its place
—Jean Matteson

4

THOUGHTS ON
ORGANIZATION

In poring over the ideas in those twenty-five books, I was
taken by the quality of the ideas contained therein.

They represent proven principles that work. A principle is a law, like gravity. A law works every time.

Here are some laws will allow you to be effective, to
work smarter, not harder. Isn't that what we all want?

- Think Japanese...SIMPLIFY!

- Remember S.H.E.D.: ELIMINATE CLUTTER
  in your life:

Separate the treasures from the trash. Slow down. Understand the attachment you have to clutter. Change your self-image.

Heave the trash. Let go of the irrelevant. That means any object or activity that depletes you.

Embrace your identity. You are not your stuff. Say it aloud: "I am not my stuff!" Discover your authentic self. Pull up your identity from within.

Drive yourself forward. Experiment with activities, experiences, and items to your theme for the future until it feels right to you.

— Julie Morganstern,
Changing from the Inside Out

- *Until you value yourself, you will not value your time. Until you value your time, you will not do anything with it.*

— Dr. M. Scott Peck, *The Road Less Traveled*

- *When your daily activities are in alignment with highest priorities, you have a credible claim to inner peace.*

— Hyrum W. Smith, FranklinCovey Institute

- *NO is not a dirty word.*

— Mark Matteson

- *Be quick, but don't hurry.*

— Coach John Wooden, UCLA

- *Scotoma* is the Greek word for "blind spot." What are your scotomas in regard to your habits, behavior, and attitudes about time?

- *What got you HERE won't take you THERE. There are some things you will need to START doing and there are some things you will need to STOP doing to reach your new goals. What are they?*

  — Mark Matteson

- In his White House office in 1864, Abraham Lincoln said to Russell Conwell, a young officer, *Young man, I am a very busy man. Tell me exactly what you want and I will do my very best to see if I can help you get it.* Wow! What an effective, firm, but kind thing to say to a friend, relative, or co-worker. He was assertive but compassionate.

- To facilitate an effective meeting, remember the 7-Point Formula:

  1. What is the meeting's objective?

  2. What question should this meeting answer?

  3. What is each participant expected to contribute?

  4. How long will this meeting last?

  5. Who will be taking notes, minutes?

  6. Summarize the TAKEAWAYS and Follow-up Actions

  7. WHO will do WHAT by WHEN?

- My good friend Chuck Orton taught me this simple formula for an effective meeting. It allows equanimity in a group setting. The people who talk the most must listen. The quiet ones must learn to contribute. In your next company meeting, remember **E.S.O.B.A.S.T.**

Everyone

Speaks

Once

Before

Anyone

Speaks

Twice

- At home or work, labeling files, shelves, or genres saves time and frustration. Make it legible.

- Clipping articles is fine, provided you have a file or box for them.

- Finding simpler ways of getting things done does not detract from the quality of the result.

- **D.I.N.** = **D**o **I**t **N**ow! Sometimes, doing something right away is the best strategy. I was at the club working out. A friend asked me whether I did any professional coaching. *Of course,* I said. We talked briefly, and he gave me the correct spelling of his first and last name, e-mail address, and phone number. I wrote it in my workout journal. When I got home that night, I entered his name into my contacts, put him in my e-zine database, and sent him an e-mail with a couple of articles I had written that were germane to his objectives. *D.I.N.* He became a client and is a joy to work with. The palest ink is better than the strongest memory. WRITE IT DOWN. Avoid trusting it to memory.

- Where performance is measured, performance improves. What if you kept a time log for a week? Track and measure what is important to you: your savings-account balance, waist size, or weekly sales.

- That was then, this is now. Why are you hanging on to certain things? Purge your wardrobe once a year. Go through your files and purge. Rearrange your office once a year. Your personal productivity will soar.

- Alphabetize. Put your books, CDs, DVDs, and files in alphabetical order for quick reference. It makes things so much easier to find.

- On the weekends, make mini-lists and prioritize. Small projects and errands require some thought if you are to be effective.

- Read a book on time management or organization once a year over the holidays or on your birthday. Give yourself that gift. See the list of books in Chapter 1.

- Declare a war on CLUTTER! Put the highest-priority item from your pile in the center of your desk and keep everything else out of sight. Remember, you can only think of one thing at a time. A word about knick-knacks, those family photos, souvenir paperweights, clocks, and trinkets that take up space: why not put them on a shelf or side table? They won't take up valuable working space and create a visual distraction. Before you end your day, clear the desk completely; it gets the next day off to a good start.

- Sometimes the answer to your goal will come when you least expect it, even in the middle of the night. Henry Kaiser made it a practice to "assign" his subconscious mind a problem to work on before going to sleep. He found the answer often came to him at around 3:00 AM, so he always kept a notepad and pen on the nightstand next to his bed. He would scribble the idea down and go back to sleep without worrying about forgetting the great idea.

- Do you find your energy and focus failing in the early afternoon? Consider a short nap, perhaps 20 minutes. Famous nappers include Edison, Churchill, Kennedy, and Einstein. When I first started in sales, I would leave the office and drive to the park. There, I would kick the seat back and close my eyes for 20 to 30 minutes. Refreshed, I returned to the office and worked for four more hours. Consider a nap your half-time. You now have in front of you the second half of your day.

- "When in doubt, throw it out!" Most of us have too many files. When you consider deleting a file, ask yourself, "If I wanted this item again someday and didn't have it, what would I do?" Excessive hoarding and record keeping is a symptom of insecurity and defensive thinking. Your thinking is in the past, not the present. "IF in doubt, throw it out." We now have the "Cloud." Store it "up there" and forget about it. God bless Apple and Google.

- A word on follow-up: If you ask people to do things and they usually don't get around to them, stop asking yourself, *What's the matter with people these days?* Instead, ask yourself, *What is wrong with ME? What am I doing (or not doing) that causes people to give me empty promises?* Chances are you have been training them to do just that. Entrust people with WHAT, WHEN, and WHY. Leave the HOW up to them. Use this effective formula:

  1. The date assigned

  2. The person responsible

  3. The action and objective

  4. The due date

  5. The completion

- When you call someone, always ask, "Do you have a minute?" or "Is this a good time?" or "How much time do we have?"

- Nordstrom uses a simple empowering philosophy. It's the company's number-one rule: *"Use your best judgment! If you have any questions, ask."* The implication is "We TRUST YOU!" Entrust others with responsibility. Reward results. Try using the following phrases: "Great Job!", "Way to go!", "You rock!", "I am proud of you!", "Now you're cooking!", "Keep it going!", "Well done!", and my personal favorite, "Your future is so bright it burns my eyes to look at it!"

- Instead of time-consuming travel, consider using Skype teleconferences (I am now conducting monthly seminars internationally and they are very effective). Check out www.FreeConferenceCall.com, webinars, or group e-mail. Use the same planning formula as an in-person meeting:

  1. How much time do we have?

  2. What is our objective?

  3. Who will be taking notes?

  4. What are the takeaways and action items?

  5. WHO will do WHAT by WHEN?

YOUR NOTES

_____

_____

_____

_____

_____

_____

_____

_____

_____

_____

_____

_____

_____

_____

_____

_____

_____

_____

_____

_____

5

On Procrastination

How many legs does this elephant have?

Take a good look at the picture on the previous page. How many legs do you see? Look again. It's confusing, isn't it? It's an optical illusion. An elephant is supposed to have four legs. How many did you count? Have you ever heard the phrase "the elephant in the room"? It means "the big issue that everyone avoids discussing." Another phrase is: "How do you eat an elephant?" Answer: Cut it up and eat it a bite at a time. An elephant project seems so overwhelming, we put off beginning because we feel overwhelmed by the sheer magnitude of the project! However many legs your elephant project has, begin by tackling just one at a time.

I recently went through my inbox and found a notice that the tags for my son's car were due. I made a mental note (big mistake), told myself, *I'll take care of it tomorrow,* (bigger mistake), and then forgot about it. Evan called me a week later to tell me he received a ticket for $124 after being stopped. The tags would have cost me $39. Procrastination comes with a price. We all do it: with big things, with little things, with unpleasant things. Well, I am trying to make NEW mistakes, not the same old ones. So, I am writing this chapter for me, to remind myself of what I need to do daily.

Procrastination wears many masks: laziness, indifference, forgetfulness, overwork. However, I believe it is usually a single word: FEAR. Analyze your fears. Precisely what are you afraid of? Is yours real or imagined? Do you fear criticism, poverty, ill-health, loss of love, death?

Ben Franklin wrote, *We procrastinate on any project that the direction is unclear and will take longer than forty-five min-*

utes. That is so true. Who procrastinates? The answer is, "each and every one of us."

It's a long and painful list: Clean out the closet, mow the lawn, do your taxes, lose thirty pounds, write that book, organize your desktop, office, or car.

What are the true emotional costs of procrastination? Doubt, fear, anxiety, resentment, self-pity, uncertainty, and lowered feelings of self-worth and self-esteem are some of the costs. They hold us back from reaching our potential. Our habits and feelings betray us.

Each of us moves toward pleasure and away from pain. It's how we are wired. I had to get real about what was holding me back. I was making excuses. I was creatively avoiding this unpleasant elephant.

As I faced my giant pachyderm head-on, I began to brainstorm in my journal for some solutions. I hope they help you. I know they will help me.

Change your belief and self-image. Write a new declaration. How about:

I keep my word to myself. I have integrity and I finish what I start. I tackle uncomfortable projects with enthusiasm. I just do it!

Repeat that affirmation five to ten times a day for thirty days!

Here is a simple formula for getting things done. Let's cut up that elephant and eat it one bite at a time.

1. Make a list in a journal of all the projects and tasks you have been putting off.

2. Prioritize the list in order of importance.

3. Take your #1 elephant and brainstorm. Ask yourself on paper:

   a) What exactly needs to be done?

   b) Why am I putting it off?

   c) What are the benefits of getting this done?

   d) What will it mean to me once I have completed this?

4. Make a long list of little action items (sub-goals) to take and rank them in order of importance.

5. Estimate how long each little action will take (e.g. twenty minutes) to the right of the item.

6. Pick a date and put it on your calendar. Two options here:

   a) Tackle it all in one day.

   b) Do an hour a day for however many days it takes to finish the task.

7. Hold yourself accountable by telling someone you respect that you will do it.

8. Determine a reward you will give yourself when you have completed this project. Make it special and significant for you.

9. Get started and do the thing you don't like first.

10. If you get stuck or frustrated, ask for help from someone who has done what you want to do and been where you want to go.

Remember when you were a kid, you ate the vegetables first? Maybe you put ketchup on them, or lots of butter, but you ate them first so you could enjoy the rest of the meal.

When I decided to write my first book *Freedom from Fear* (available at www.SparkingSuccess.net) eleven years ago, I got up at 5 am every day for a month. I wrote first thing in the morning, three pages or for two hours, whichever came first. I have done that with every book I have written. I am doing it with the one I am writing now, three pages a day or for one hour, whichever comes first. It's amazing. The book is 75 percent complete. It writes itself.

Consider these words from great achievers about time and procrastination:

We shall never have more time. We have, and always had, all the time there is. No object is served in waiting until next week or even until tomorrow. Keep going. Concentrate on something useful.

> — Arnold Bennett, from the book
> *How to Live on 24 Hours a Day*

Do the thing you fear and the death of fear is certain.

> — William James,
> father of American psychology

How soon "Not Now" becomes "NEVER."

— Elbert Hubbard,
publisher, author

Procrastination is the grave in which opportunity is buried.

— Neil Armstrong,
astronaut, author, speaker

Finish every day and be done with it. You have done what you could. Some blunders and absurdities no doubt crept in; forget them as soon as you can. Tomorrow is a new day; begin it well and serenely and with too high a spirit to be cumbered with your old nonsense. This day is all that is good and fair. It is too dear, with its hopes and invitations, to waste a moment on yesterdays.

— Ralph Waldo Emerson,
philosopher, essayist, author

An adventure is the deliberate, volitional movement out of the comfort zone.

— James W. Newman, author of
Release Your Brakes!

Fear not that life shall come to an end, but rather fear that it shall never have a beginning.

— Cardinal John Henry Newman

Is it time to acknowledge the elephant in your living room? Hand me that knife—I have some carving to do!

YOUR NOTES

_____

_____

_____

_____

_____

_____

_____

_____

_____

_____

_____

_____

_____

_____

_____

_____

_____

_____

_____

6

ON VALUES AND GOALS

Roy Disney, Walt's brother, said, "When your values are clear, decisions are simple." What are your values? What would you stand up for? What would you lay down your life for?

When the fifty-six men who signed the Declaration of Independence put their signatures on that document, they knew one of two things would happen: they would die or be free from British tyranny. Most of them were gentleman farmers, entrepreneurs who donated their time to political pursuits because they believed in the cause of liberty.

My good friend Andrew Bennett told me in 1993, *Show me your checkbook and your day planner, and I will tell you what YOU value!* How do you spend your time and money? THAT is the clearest and most accurate measure of your values.

> *If we are to go forward, we must go back and rediscover those precious values—that all reality hinges on moral foundations and that all reality has spiritual control.*
>
> — Martin Luther King, Jr.,
> civil rights leader

> *So when these people sell out, even though they get fabulously rich, they're gypping themselves out of one of the potentially most rewarding experiences of their unfolding lives. Without it, they may never know their values or how to keep their newfound wealth in perspective.*
>
> — Steve Jobs,
> co-founder of Apple

My Twelve Governing VALUES are:

1. _____

   _____

2. _____

   _____

3. _____

   _____

4. _____

_____

5. _____

_____

6. _____

_____

7. _____

_____

8. _____

_____

9. _____

_____

10. _____

_____

11. _____

_____

12. _____

_____

I found that VALUES, for each person, were numerous. Therefore, I proposed to write my VALUE names and annex to each a short precept—which fully expressed the extent I gave each meaning. I then arranged them in such a way as to facilitate acquisition of these virtues.

—*The Autobiography of Benjamin Franklin*

SAMPLE VALUES

- *I am teachable and humble.*

- *I am frugal.*

- *I am industrious and work smart each day in alignment with my values and goals.*

- *I have integrity and I keep my word to myself first, to others second.*

MY TOP 50 TOTAL LIFETIME GOALS ARE: (WHAT DO YOU WANT TO BE?)

1. _____

_____

2. _____

_____

3. _____

_____

4. _____

_____

5. _____

_____

6. _____

_____

7. _____

_____

8. _____

_____

9. _____

_____

10. _____

_____

SAMPLE IDEAS

- *A bestselling author of twenty books*

- *A 5-handicap in golf*

- *A great-grandfather, alive at 105 and in terrific health*

- *A real estate owner, flipping a house every other year*
- *A world-class international speaker*
- *A season ticket holder to Seattle Supersonics (oops, OKC Thunder)*
- *A fluent Spanish speaker*
- *A Servant Leader, a kind and loving father and husband*
- *A fly fisherman (hey, wait a minute—that's my wife!)*

WHAT DO YOU WANT TO HAVE?

1. _____
   _____

2. _____
   _____

3. _____
   _____

4. _____
   _____

5. _____
   _____

6. _____

_____

7. _____

_____

8. _____

_____

9. _____

_____

10. _____

_____

SAMPLE IDEAS

- *Joy and peace of mind*
- *Financial independence*
- *Happy, successful, and well-adjusted children*
- *Healthy and meaningful relationships at work and at home*
- *A second home on Lake Chelan as a getaway two months of the year*
- *Zero debt and $100,000 in savings and another $100,000 in mutual funds and CDs*
- *All my vehicles paid for*

WHAT DO YOU WANT TO SEE?

1. _____
   _____

2. _____
   _____

3. _____
   _____

4. _____
   _____

5. _____
   _____

6. _____
   _____

7. _____
   _____

8. _____
   _____

9. _____
   _____

10. _____

_____

Sample Ideas

- *Australia: Sydney Harbor, Melbourne, Argue with a kangaroo in the wild!*

- *Istanbul: Topkapi Palace, the Blue Mosque, The Grand Bazaar*

- *Niagara Falls on the Canadian Side*

- *Mexico: Mazatlán, Puerto Vallarta, Cancún, Cozumel*

- *Hawaii: Hike Diamond Head, Dinner at Sam Choy's, Surf North Shore*

- *Arizona: Hike Camelback at Sunrise, Visit Sedona and buy art*

- *Stehekin on the west end of Lake Chelan: Rainbow Falls*

- *Egypt: the Nile at sunset and the Pyramids at sunrise*

- *Chateau Lake Louise and Banff in Canada*

What do you want to DO?

1. _____

_____

2. _____

_____

3. _____
   _____

4. _____
   _____

5. _____
   _____

6. _____
   _____

7. _____
   _____

8. _____
   _____

9. _____
   _____

10. _____
    _____

SAMPLE IDEAS

- *Climb Mt. Rainier with my family*
- *Learn to play the piano*

- *Write a #1 hit song*

- *Tour the United States on a book tour with my grandkids*

- *Make a hole-in-one in golf*

- *Do a book tour in Japan*

- *Visit Ben and Jerry's ice cream plant in Stowe, Vermont*

- *Visit Teddy Roosevelt's home, Sagamore Hill, on Long Island*

- *Visit Monticello, Thomas Jefferson's home in Virginia*

- *Visit The Liberty Bell in Philadelphia*

- *Fish for halibut in Homer, Alaska*

- *Skydive and live to write about it*

- *See an NBA game in every city (I am up to eight!)*

WHAT DO YOU WANT TO SHARE?

1. _____

   _____

2. _____

   _____

3. _____

   _____

4. _____

_____

5. _____

_____

6. _____

_____

7. _____

_____

8. _____

_____

9. _____

_____

10. _____

_____

SAMPLE IDEAS

- *Write ten bestselling children's books and donate the proceeds to a literacy organization*

- *Conduct FREE open seminars in prisons*

- *Conduct seminars for college sports teams and keynote sports banquets*

- *Help other speakers and authors get their books published and become bestselling authors and speakers worldwide*

Life is not measured by the number of breaths we take, but by the places and moments that take our breath away!

— Patricia Schultz, author,
1,000 Places to See Before You Die

My Top Ten Goals for This Year are:

1. _____

_____

2. _____

_____

3. _____

_____

4. _____

_____

5. _____

_____

6. _____

_____

7. _____

_____

8. _____

_____

9. _____

_____

10. _____

_____

KEYS TO EFFECTIVE GOAL PLANNING

1. *Supported by your governing values*

2. *Time Dimensioned*

3. *Clearly and specifically defined*

4. *Take ownership of the goal—make it yours*

5. *Realistic, but stretches your existing comfort zones*

The goal statement helps bring your future into the present by giving you a clearer view of what your ideal future looks like.

— Alan Lakein, author of
How to Gain Control of Your time and Your Life

SELF-IMAGE

According to the Cleveland Clinic, self-image is the personal view we have of ourselves. It is our mental image or self-portrait. Self-image is an internal dictionary that describes the characteristics of the self, including intelligent, beautiful, ugly, talented, selfish, and kind. These characteristics form a collective representation of our assets and liabilities as we see them.

Think of your self-image as being like a thermostat in your head. If the t-stat is set for 70 degrees, it will maintain that temperature within a dead band, or margin, of four degrees. If the room temperature drops below 68 degrees, the t-stat sends a 24-volt signal to bring on the heat. If the temperature should rise above 72 degrees, the t-stat sends a signal for cooling. The air-conditioning will come on and maintain a comfort zone within that dead band setting.

You have a Comfort Zone in all areas of your life: the kind of driver you are, how much money you like to keep in the bank, how much you earn each year, the kind of athlete you are, and so on. The list is endless. So why is this important? Because YOU control the setting! Growing up, it was authorities—parents, relatives, teachers, coaches, and "popular" kids—who controlled the settings with constant observation and reports. It was formed by the words others used to describe your behavior and attitude.

During my sophomore year in high school in 1973, a very dynamic and inspirational former state championship basketball coach and psychology teacher came to speak at an assembly. His words lit a fire under me. I asked the principal whether more information was available. He handed me a brochure: *ACTION FOR EXCELLENCE, $45, TWO-DAY SEMINAR.* I sold my mother on the idea of writing a check and driving me to Seattle University for the weekend. It changed my life forever.

Using the tools Bob Moawad shared that weekend, I changed my thermostat setting and went from scrub to basketball star in three weeks. I created a new Comfort Zone by setting, affirming aloud, and visualizing my basketball goals. It was magic.

The truth is, every goal I have ever set from then until now was a lie at the beginning; nothing was further from the truth until I accomplished it. And my belief that I could achieve that goal (and consequently did) was a direct result of proving to myself I could do it as demonstrated by my early basketball success. My next success was with my grades. In college, I enjoyed a 3.8 G.P.A. without gritting my teeth or trying hard. My self-image did the work. It maintained my new Comfort Zone.

You can do the same thing. Would you like to increase your income by 20 to 30 percent? Become a more effective parent or spouse? Write a book? Improve your public speaking skills? Have a positive attitude? Improve every relationship in your life? Embrace technology and have fun doing it?

Make a list of five areas in your life and career you would like to improve.

1. _____

_____

2. _____

_____

3. _____

_____

4. _____

_____

5. _____

_____

Now choose one area to concentrate on.

_____

_____

_____

_____

_____

_____

_____

_____

We gain the strength of the temptation we resist.
— Ralph Waldo Emerson

Our acts make or mar us; we are the children of our own deeds.
— Victor Hugo

When you have to make a choice and don't make it, that is in itself a choice.
— William James

Your #1 Goal for This Year Is?

_____

_____

_____

_____

_____

_____

_____

_____

Five Reasons Why You Want to Achieve That Goal:

1. _____

_____

2. _____

_____

3. _____

_____

4. _____

_____

5. _____

_____

The strangest secret in the world is WE BECOME WHAT WE THINK ABOUT!

> — Earl Nightingale, author and
> pioneer of audio learning

Is what I am doing moving me toward one of my top ten goals?

> — Ed Bliss, author of
> *Getting Things Done*

Accept the full gift of this moment; you deserve it. Take hold of today. Use it, enjoy it in the most exciting, creative way you can. This is the day for you to do the things that are most important to you. This is the day to know how good it is to be alive.

> — Dru Scott, author of
> *How to Put More Time in Your Life*

What Are the Six Most Important Things I Need to Do Today?

1. _____

_____

2. _____
   _____

3. _____
   _____

4. _____
   _____

5. _____
   _____

Monthly "Grass Catcher" (Random but vital action items).

_____

_____

_____

_____

_____

_____

_____

_____

"Life is the sum of all your choices."

— Albert Camus

7

THE SELF-CONFIDENCE
FORMULA

In the early decades of the 20th century, Napoleon Hill identified and set down on paper some of the keystones of success. Here, paraphrased from his original language, is his *Self-Confidence Formula...*

> *I know I have the ability to achieve the object of my definite chief aim and purpose in life; therefore, I demand of myself persistent continuous action toward its attainment, and I here and now promise to render such action!*

I realize the dominating thoughts of my mind will even-tually reproduce themselves in outward, physical action, and gradually transform themselves into physical real-ity; therefore, I will concentrate my thoughts for thirty minutes a day upon the task of thinking on paper of the person I intend to become, thereby creating in my mind a clear and exciting mental picture! (For ninety days I will write my #1 Goal out in my journal and wait for the ideas and road signs that will inevitably come to me in my morning THINK sessions).

I know through the principle of autosuggestion (declar-ing and affirming aloud), any desire that I persistently hold in my mind will eventually seek expression through some practical means of attaining the object I seek; there-fore, I will devote ten minutes daily to demanding of myself this development of self-confidence!

I have clearly written down a description of my definite chief aim in life and I will never stop trying until I shall develop sufficient self-confidence for its attainment!

I fully realize that no wealth or position can long endure unless built upon truth and justice; therefore, I will engage in no transaction which does not benefit all whom it affects. I will succeed by attracting to myself the forces I wish to use and the cooperation of other people. I will induce others to serve me because of my willingness to serve others first and enthusiastically.

I will eliminate hatred, envy, resentment, self-pity, criti-cism/judgment/cynicism/ridicule, selfishness, and impa-tience by developing a true love for all of humanity because I know that a negative attitude toward others can never bring me success. I will cause others to believe in me because I will believe in them and in myself. I will sign my name to this formula, commit it to memory, and read it aloud once a day for ninety days with full faith that it will gradually influence my thoughts and actions, so I will become confident, grateful, wealthy, and a successful professional.

* * *

Don't be afraid of death so much as an inadequate life.

— Bertolt Brecht

It is while you are patiently toiling at the little tasks of life that the meaning and shape of the great whole of life dawns on you.

— Phillips Brooks

One's philosophy is not best expressed in words; it's expressed in the choices one makes.

— Eleanor Roosevelt

ACTIONS YOU ARE INSPIRED TO TAKE?

_____

_____

_____

_____

_____

_____

It's About TIME

8

Seven Deadly Sins of Effective Communication

We can be effective in our use of time and talent, yet if we ignore how we interact with others, our effectiveness will be diminished. Strained relations have an enormous opportunity cost in business and in life. Below you will find the *Seven Deadly Sins of Effective Communication* and their *Seven Positive Antidotes for Effective Communication*. The habitual use of the latter disciplines will dramatically increase morale, productivity, and bottom-line performance.

Seven Deadly Sins of Effective Communication

1. **Appearing uninterested when someone else is talking:** no eye contact, looking at your phone, sending a text or e-mail, etc. How do you feel when someone does that to you? What if you gave the other person the gift of attention and respect you would want?

2. **Talking too much about you.** Fellas, more often than not, we are guilty of this. Women seem to have an advantage here, as they are ever mindful of equanimity in dialogue. What if we were as mindful?

3. **Telling long, pointless stories.** This is all ego and fear. No one wants to be left out. What if you were mindful of why you are telling a story and how long it goes on?

4. **Criticizing, arguing, disputing, and disagreeing with someone directly.** (It becomes ten times worse when done in public!) This is a giant faux pas. Would you rather be right or happy?

5. **Ridiculing someone in public.** Unless you are in politics, stay away from ridicule like you would rabies.

6. **Interrupting or correcting others.** This habit also has its roots in self-centered fear: fear you

won't get what you want or you will lose what you have. What if you bit your tongue instead?

7. **Gossip.** I have saved the worst for last. I had to learn this one the hard way in my early thirties. The ripple effect of criticizing someone behind his back lasted over ten years and caused me a great deal of grief, bad blood, time, and sleepless nights.

SEVEN POSITIVE ANTIDOTES FOR EFFECTIVE COMMUNICATION

1. **Show sincere interest in what others have to say.** Pay attention; honor them with eye contact; nod, smile, and occasionally say, "Uh-huh," "Really?" and "No...Then what happened?" The results are astonishing. Besides, I never learned anything when I was talking!

2. **Be aware of how much talking you are actually doing.** Monitor your part in every conversation. Think of it as a spotlight on the celebrity. You are the reporter. You ask questions and listen. Resist the temptation to say, *That's nothing; one time I...* Instead, say, *Yes, and then what happened?* Magic!

3. **Listen actively.** When it is your time to contribute, tell a germane story that is short, has a specific point, and then wait and watch the reaction. I prefer two categories of stories: a) First Person Warnings (where I am the punch

line, using self-effacing humor, as was Ben Franklin's habit); b) Third Person Examples (where a client or friend changed and prospered). They seem to be very well-received. Avoid the word YOU.

4. **Get in the habit of saying, "That's an interesting point of view."** or "You feel strongly about that." Then wait and watch. The person's position may soften.

5. **Remain silent.** Silence is extremely difficult for most people. Nod, smile, and even take notes. When it is your time to talk, see the advice in #3. "It's best to remain silent and risk being thought a fool, than to talk and remove all doubt!"

6. **Let others finish their stories.** Your time will come. Be patient. Resist the urge to *one up* the other person. Paraphrase what you hear and be quiet again. You will be amazed how people will open up to you and tell you things they don't tell their barber, banker, or best friend.

7. **Upon hearing gossip, smile, nod, and simply say, "It sounds like you disagree or dislike his position or behavior. Let's go talk to him together to sort this out."** Most of the time, the person will vehemently deny his position. However, one thing is certain: he will stop gossiping to YOU. The rumor mill will shut down.

A broken limb is often stronger after it has healed, but the same thing rarely happens with fractured relationships. After a relationship fracture, the break lingers below the surface, and can completely collapse under a subsequent stress.

— Dr. Mardy Grothe

IF I COULD JUST GET ORGANIZED

There may be nothing wrong with you,

The way you live, the work you do,

But I can very plainly see,

Exactly what is wrong with me.

It isn't that I'm indolent;

I work as hard as anyone,

And yet I get so little done,

The morning goes, the noon is here,

Before I know, the night is near,

And all around me, I regret,

Are things I haven't finished yet.

If I could just get organized!

I oftentimes have realized

Not all that matters is the man;

The man must also have a plan.

With you, there may be nothing wrong,

But here's my trouble right along;

I do the things that don't amount

To very much, of no account,

That really seem important though

And let a lot of matters go.

I nibble this, I nibble that,

But never finish what I'm at.

I work as hard as anyone,

And yet, I get so little done,

I'd do so much you'd be surprised,

If I could just get organized!

— Douglas Malloch

9

ON ATTITUDE

A quote I have been reading in my seminars for almost twenty years comes from author, pastor, and philosopher Chuck Swindoll. It has, quite frankly, changed my attitude. It has also served to move this wonderful quality into the top three aspects of my character that I most cherish. I need reminding a lot. Here it is:

ATTITUDE

The longer I live, the more I realize the impact of Attitude on life. Attitude to me is more important than the past, than education, than money, than circumstances, than failures, than successes, than what other people think, say or do. It's more important than appearance, giftedness, or skill. It will make or break a company, a church, or a home. The remarkable thing is we have a choice every single day regarding the Attitude we will embrace for that day. We cannot change the past, we cannot change the fact that people will act in a certain way. The only thing we can do is play on the string we have, and that string is our Attitude. I am convinced that life is 10% what happens to me, and 90% how I respond to it. I am in charge of my Attitude.

— Chuck Swindoll, author, pastor

Companies rise and fall in their customers' favor for a variety of reasons. The American Society for Quality Control reports the following study showing the relative importance of several reasons companies lose customers:

Died. 1%

Moved away. 3%

Influenced by friends. 5%

Lured away by the competition. 9%

Dissatisfied with product 14%

Employee indifference toward customer 68%

The emphasis on good service has increased so much of late that the ASQC warns: *Unless a customer is completely satisfied—to the point of being positively delighted and willing to brag about the product or service received—there exists great potential for market damage and future trouble for the company.*

Make up your mind that you are going to have a good attitude for as long as you live—I have no use for a sour-faced man. Furthermore, commit to working smart and finish what you start.

> — Franklin Robinson, from the book
> *A Simple Choice* by Mark Matteson

Did you know ATTITUDE, more than almost any other characteristic, will determine your success or failure in any endeavor? We do have a choice, every single day.

Webster's Dictionary defines attitude as: *a settled way of thinking or feeling, typically reflected in a person's behavior; a position of the body proper to or implying an action or mental state; manner, disposition with regard to a person or thing; tendency or orientation.*

Albert Einstein said, *Weakness of attitude becomes weakness of character.*

Winston Churchill said, *Attitude is a little thing that makes a big difference.*

Maya Angelou wrote, *If you don't like something, change it. If you can't change it, change your attitude.*

Thomas Jefferson affirmed, *Nothing can stop the man with the right mental attitude from achieving his goal; nothing on earth can help the man with the wrong attitude.*

Joel Osteen said, *Choosing to be positive and having a grateful attitude is going to determine how you are going to live your life.*

Teddy Roosevelt wrote, *The reactionary is always willing to take a progressive attitude on any issue that is dead.*

Here is a list of twelve simple things anyone can do to change his or her attitude. They work. I know because I am a recovering pessimist.

1. Read biographies and autobiographies of successful people every day, even if it's only for fifteen minutes. Start your day the right way.

2. Associate with people who have great attitudes: positive, enthusiastic, kind, caring people who have the qualities you seek. Their attitude will infect yours in a positive way, quickly.

3. Keep a journal of WINS. When something great happens in your life, write it down. Describe in detail the positive aspects of the event, especially how you felt about it.

4. Make a gratitude list. What are the things for which you are grateful? Your health, family, good friends, meaning in your work, your hometown or community? List them!

5. Listen to educational and inspirational audio programs on CDs and MP3s. "Windshield University" will inspire and instruct. I have earned the equivalent of two university degrees by listening to audio books for the last twenty years. Stop listening to music all the time. Plug into the minds of your mentors!

6. Ask positive people what they do to maintain such a great attitude. Write it down. Model that behavior. Why reinvent the wheel?

7. Find mentors, people who have done what you want to do and been where you want to go. Meet with them on a regular basis. Did you know your income is an average of the five people with whom you spend the most time? I created a board of directors with twenty-five people both living and dead who have inspired me, like Thomas Jefferson. I think about them, quote them, and read about them and what they have taught me on a regular basis. Their pictures are on the wall in my office.

8. Make a *Notable Accomplishment List.* Go back through your history and list all the great things you have done: straight A's in junior high, hitting the winning shot in high school, Eagle Scout; you get the idea. This simple exercise will feed your soul and build your confidence and self-worth.

9. Pray and meditate every day. Prayer is talking to God; meditation is listening.

10. CHOOSE to have a great Attitude. You can start your day over any time you want to.

11. Take a thirty-day vacation from the media. Stop listening to talk radio and the news. Give up TV and newspapers. It's 90 percent bad

news. Bad news sells newspapers. Have you ever been on vacation when you didn't have any exposure to all that negativity? How did you feel? Simple, isn't it? Garbage in, garbage out. Manage your input.

12. Examine your self-talk. Really listen. The average person has 60,000 thoughts a day. According to experts, 75 percent of those thoughts are negative! Pay attention to your reactions to the world around you. There are three components to self-talk:

 a) Thoughts you hold silently.

 b) Words you say aloud to yourself.

 c) Words you say to others.

Ty Cobb, the legendary baseball icon, had a lifetime batting average of .366. When asked by a reporter what he thought he would hit when he was seventy years old, he replied, *"Oh, .290, .300."*

"Oh," the reporter replied. "That's because of astro turf, night games, 95 mph fastballs, and sliders?"

Pausing for a moment, Cobb replied, "NO! It's because I'm seventy!" THAT's the right attitude!

STEP BY STEP

I ask questions, I read, I listen. I'm not afraid to ask anybody anything if I don't know. Why should I be afraid? I'm trying to get somewhere. Help me, give me direction.

Nothing wrong with that. Step by step, I can't see any other way of accomplishing anything.

— Michael Jordan, NBA icon

Everybody, soon or late, sits down to a banquet of consequences.

— Robert Louis Stevenson

You aspire to do great things? Begin with little ones.

— Saint Augustine

Each day, and the living of it, has to be a conscious creation in which discipline and order are relieved with some play and pure foolishness.

— May Sarton

WHAT WILL YOU DO TO IMPROVE YOUR ATTITUDE?

1. _____

   _____

2. _____

   _____

3. _____

   _____

4. _____

   _____

5. _____

_____

6. _____

_____

If you don't get everything you want, think of the things you don't get that you don't want.

— Oscar Wilde

If you don't think every day is a good day, just try missing one.

— Cavett Robert, founder of
the National Speakers Association

10

ANTHROPOMAXIMOLOGY?

D r. Charles Garfield coined the term, "anthropomax-
imology" in his book Peak Performers. He was part
of the Apollo Moon Program, his team responsible for
the lunar module the astronauts would use on the moon.
He said,

> I have never seen a team of people be transformed as
> that group in the mid-sixties. Every night as we left work
> after 12-hour days, we would all look up at the moon.
> THAT was the goal. We were energized, passionate, and
> all became so much more than any of us had been prior
> to that mission. When it was over, miraculously in a
> sad way, almost everyone went back to being average.
> It's like someone flipped a switch. I did not understand

what had happened. So I went back to school and studied Peak Performance. I earned a second doctorate and wrote about what I learned.

Passion and preference: Peak Performers do what unsuccessful people are unwilling to do. They focus on making a difference in the world. They find a need and fill it. They listen to the marketplace and then pour themselves into creating products or services to fill that need. They become experts in their fields.

Viktor E. Frankl's story of redemption and perseverance, recorded in his book *Man's Search for Meaning*, has changed my point of view on two separate occasions. Victor was captured and imprisoned by the Nazis during World War II. He lost his wife, mother, father, and sister. Frankl describes in extraordinary detail exactly how he survived Auschwitz and the atrocities all around him. While a prisoner, he set about serving others and came to the simple realization that his captors could take everything away, except for one simple thing. He writes:

The last of the great human freedoms is our ability to choose our response in any given set of circumstances. It was the one thing my captors could not take away from me.

In short, it came down to how he responded to what was happening to him and around him! He found strength, courage, and meaning in all the suffering. His experiences and insights formed the basis of a process he called logotherapy: his belief that all life has meaning no matter the circumstances. This belief kept him alive. It gave him purpose and meaning. At night, before falling asleep, he would visualize himself speaking to thousands of students recalling how he survived the death camp. He not only survived, he created a model for overcoming adversity of the worst kind. He left an enduring legacy.

If you find yourself frustrated, down and out, feeling like a victim, or feeling sorry for yourself, read *Man's Search for Meaning*. When you put it down, you will be a different person—I promise.

So, How Does the Mind Work?

Self-image psychology exploded onto the scene with Dr. Maxwell Maltz's 1960 international bestseller *Psycho-Cybernetics*. As a plastic surgeon, he was astonished, baffled even, by the lack of change in his clients AFTER their surgery. People with severe facial disfigurements who had reconstructive surgery and had gone from gruesome to beautiful were not able to make the transition ON THE INSIDE. Perplexed, he studied the matter extensively and wrote a treatise, *How to Change from the Inside Out*. His motives were pure, his science sound, and lo and behold, dramatic changes followed for his patients in their attitude, behavior, self-esteem, self-worth, and performance.

Remember: *All meaningful and lasting change begins first on the inside and works its way out.*

L.S. Barksdale wrote in 1972, *A happy, zestful life is indeed an attainable goal. It's not what happens to us, but how we handle it that determines our misery or well-being.* The information in this book is about being well. We CAN have it all—prosperity, abundance, peace of mind, joy, respect, and balance: a sense of adequacy, self-worth, self-respect, and self-esteem. Those last three: worth, respect, and esteem form a kind of triangle of the self-concept.

Much of our unhappiness comes from a lack of awareness. We simply don't know. There are five levels or stages of competence.

STAGE ONE - UNCONSCIOUS INCOMPETENCE

We don't know that we don't know. We are clueless in Seattle (or wherever you live). In this first stage, we are blissfully unaware of our ignorance. Ignorance is not bliss. An absence of knowledge, attitude, skills, or habits is the worst kind of poverty. The first time I had my own camera was in London at age eleven. I used the whole roll of film—twenty photographs—to take pictures of animals. My big sister tried to warn me. When I paid to have the pictures developed, they were a huge disappointment. She just laughed. That was Stage One, Unconscious Incompetence.

STAGE TWO - CONSCIOUS INCOMPETENCE

We know we don't know. This knowledge is the beginning of change. Some intrepid and caring friend says to you, *You don't have a clue!* or *Why did you say that?* It's a wake-up call of sorts. There was a time in my life, in my late teens and early twenties, where it was more important for me to be right than to be happy. One fine day, a friend called me on it. I woke up. I didn't change right away, but I knew I soon had to. In London, I had taken photos of animals instead of my loved ones and I regretted it. It was a painful learning model: *bad judgment, experience,* and finally *good judgment.*

Stage Three - Conscious Competence

We know we know. A measure of skill, focus, concentration, and teach-ability exists. We do some homework. We talk to others about how to improve. We ask questions. We take notes. We try new things. My second camera was more expensive and took better pictures. I became more selective about my choices and made certain the sun was behind me in shots I took. At night, I made certain I was not too far away for the flash to work effectively. The quality of my pictures improved. I even received a few compliments. Mind you, I was not winning any awards, but I was making progress. They were pictures worth seeing.

Stage Four - Unconscious Competence

We turn our behavior over to the subconscious. The work becomes easier, habitual, and less stressful. We operate on instinct and habit. I began carrying my camera with me and taking shots I knew would look good. I invested in a really nice camera. Just when I thought I was making progress, my wife showed me her Yashica 35mm camera and taught me how to use it. Wow, did the picture quality improve. I considered entering some of my pictures in contests. I kept the best ones in a binder. Someone said to me, "You have a great eye." That was Stage Four.

STAGE FIVE -
UNCONSCIOUS CONSCIOUS COMPETENCE

We finally arrive at a unique and fulfilling stage, *mastery*. We don't have to think about being good at something; we simply act. We are able to effectively teach what we know to others. Our knowledge is broad and extensive, our skills world-class, and our attitude positive, enthusiastic, empowering. Our habits are second nature. My pictures are ready for public consumption. Positive feedback is the norm. Time and tide have washed away all the bad judgment. What remains is worthy of note. Stage Five is a wonderful place to be. A picture is worth 1,000 words!

Beach in Aruba.

Cactus in New Mexico.

Self-portrait on Lopez Island, Washington.

What are the areas of life where you feel there is room for improvement? Financial? Physical? Interpersonal? Spiritual? Family? Choose one area and set some goals around that.

The spring quarter of my sophomore year of high school I earned a 1.8 G.P.A., including an "F" in English. My father hit the roof. He said, "Son, you are smarter than that."

He proceeded to tell me a cautionary tale—a Third-Person Warning!—about his senior year in high school. The head football coach of Ohio State University came to his school and offered him a full scholarship as a tight end. "Now Bob," Coach Carroll Widdoes said to my father in the spring of 1945, "let's see your transcripts." After reviewing his grades, he simply shook his head and said, "Sorry, son; I must rescind my offer. Maybe Bowling Green will accept you."

It was an academic wake-up call from my father. After hearing his story, I set a goal to have a 3.2 G.P.A. I wrote my goal on a 3 x 5 card and looked at it every day for a month, said it aloud many times during the day, and most importantly, visualized it at night before going to sleep. A funny thing happened that next month. I began to notice who the smart kids were. I followed one of them into the library. I had never been in there before! My friend, Katie, waved me over to a table of really smart kids and extended the invitation to join them. I did. Later, I walked her to her locker. She took the books OUT of the locker. I thought lockers were for storage! She helped me organize my stuff. She became a mentor. I began taking notes in class. I joined other study groups. I teamed up with smart kids and made myself accountable. I read the assignments, wrote the papers, and turned them in on time. When my fall report card came out during my junior year, I had a 3.2 G.P.A.

I set a new goal my senior year, changing the 3.2 to a 3.8 on my 3 x 5 card. I miraculously managed a 3.8 G.P.A. in high school my senior year and in college. You see, my self-image changed. I found a new thermostat setting, a new Comfort Zone! (Thanks, Dad.)

11

ON WORDS

Twitter is teaching us we need to think twice and speak once or not at all. Just ask Voula Papachristou, the Greek track star who tweeted a racist remark and was kicked off her country's Olympic team. Years of hard work and future fame and wealth were wiped out in a single sentence. Silence is golden. Ask Voula.

We all need reminding that words are simply tools. They can build or destroy, empower or shred, inspire or kill our dreams. What words do you habitually use and why? They lift us up or drag us down.

Would you allow someone to come into your house and dump a bag of week-old garbage in your living room and then leave? Absurd, isn't it? Yet, don't we do just that when we allow someone to gossip, criticize us, be sarcastic, shout or swear at us, or lie to us?

As stated previously, we have 60,000 thoughts a day rolling around in our brain, and 75 percent of those thoughts are negative. Why? We allow "garbage" in. Television, radio, billboards, Internet, people, books, and magazines are constantly bombarding us with negative messages. We choose to let it all in. What if you monitored your input for one day? What if you took a media break for a week as a test?

What do you say when someone asks you, "How are you?" What is your habitual response? I was on an elevator in Dallas about to give a presentation to 600 people. I asked a fellow who got on, "How are you today?" He sighed as if he were trying to get every molecule of air out of his lungs, hung his head, and said, "Okay, I guess." He didn't bother to ask me back. I felt sorry for him. He didn't understand the effect his words and attitude were having on his day, week, month, year, and life.

When I ask the question, "How are you today?" in my public seminars, I hear: "Not bad for a Monday," "Fair to middling," or "Fine" with a tone that tells me otherwise.

What if you chose a different response for a week? How about: "Fantastic!" or "Tremendous!" or "A notch above Awesome!" Does that make you feel uncomfortable? I understand. How about: "Really good!" or "Grateful" or "Great?"

Personally, I am fond of what my friend, Doug, at ninety-two years young, used to say: "I am so old, I don't even buy green bananas anymore!"

My personal favorite is "Fluctuating...between fabulous and incredible, but I haven't had my coffee yet, so I expect it to get better!" and "The best is yet to come!" That is how I sign every book I sell. I have written that phrase thousands of times. Guess what? Lennon and McCartney were right: "It's getting better all the time."

Words trigger pictures and bring about emotion. They predict and perpetuate our day's success or failure. What words are you using on a regular basis? For one week, pay attention to the words you hear others using. Write them down. Who says what? Who uses words to great effect?

WHAT WORDS DO YOU HEAR IN THE MARKETPLACE?

_____

_____

_____

_____

_____

_____

_____

_____

Read the following words aloud:

(-) Negative Words - A to Z

- ☐ Agony
- ☐ Burn
- ☐ Crash
- ☐ Death
- ☐ Explode
- ☐ Fire
- ☐ Gouge
- ☐ Hate
- ☐ Idiot
- ☐ Jealous
- ☐ Kill
- ☐ Lie
- ☐ Murder
- ☐ Negative
- ☐ Overrun
- ☐ Prison
- ☐ Quit
- ☐ Revenge
- ☐ Suffer
- ☐ Tragedy

- ☐ Ugly
- ☐ Victim
- ☐ Worry
- ☐ Xenophobe
- ☐ Yuck
- ☐ Zit (Okay, it's gross, but hey, this is an ugly list!)

NOW CHOOSE FIVE WORDS FROM THIS LIST AND CREATE A SENTENCE.

_____

_____

_____

_____

_____

_____

_____

_____

How do you feel? Pretty bad, huh? Strange, isn't it? They are just words. No big deal, right? Wrong. Words we habitually use matter. They create a mood, a feeling, an expectation, an attitude.

Now, read THESE words aloud:

(+) Positive Words - A to Z

- ☐ Achieve
- ☐ Baby
- ☐ Courage
- ☐ Deserve
- ☐ Enthusiasm
- ☐ Forgive
- ☐ Grow
- ☐ Happy
- ☐ Improve
- ☐ Joy
- ☐ Kiss
- ☐ Love
- ☐ Mend
- ☐ Nice
- ☐ Optimistic
- ☐ Positive
- ☐ Quiet
- ☐ Respect
- ☐ Smile
- ☐ Trust

☐ Understand

☐ Vacation

☐ Win

☐ Xerox (Not too many choices with the letter X! Copy that.)

☐ Yes

☐ Zeal

NOW CHOOSE FIVE WORDS FROM THIS LIST AND CREATE A SENTENCE.

_____

_____

_____

_____

_____

_____

_____

_____

How do you feel now? Better? Excited? Empowered? Crazy, huh? Yet so simple. Words matter.

Let me be very clear: I am writing this chapter as a reminder to myself. I seek to become a great mental manager. I am a work in progress. The good news is I am aware!

Here is an exercise that will be one of the hardest things you will ever try, yet at first glance, it seems so simple. Avoid complaining about anything for a whole day. That's right, no whining, sarcasm, negativity, blaming, or complaining for 24 hours. According to Hal Urban's enlightening 2004 book, *Positive Words, Powerful Results*, he threw down a challenge to over 80,000 people over the last thirty years to go 24 hours without complaining. How many do you think were able to do it? Five! That's right, five people. That is .0000625 percent of the participants! Evidently, complaining is not only a habit, but it's ingrained. Holy mackerel!

A study was done in the 1960s with barracudas and Spanish mackerel. You see, barracudas love mackerel. They are their favorite food. A group of scientists put some barracudas in a tank of water with a Plexiglas divider. On the other side were the prized mackerels. When the barracudas saw the mackerel dropped into the tank, they swam like crazy to eat them. They ran smack dab into the Plexiglas. This behavior went on for a couple of days. After hitting their noses on the Plexiglas repeatedly, the barracudas eventually figured out exactly where the partition was and would swim right up to it and then abruptly turn just before they would hit it. The scientists then removed the Plexiglas. No barrier. However, the barracudas had been conditioned. They would race right up to where the Plexiglas had been and abruptly turn and swim back. They were conditioned to avoid pain. The next day, the scientist dropped a new barracuda into the tank and he proceeded to gobble up the mackerels in ten minutes. The first group of barracudas continued to go hungry. The new guy, of course, didn't know what the others had come to know.

What "truths" are holding you back from realizing your potential? We are born to win, conditioned to lose.

Pay attention to the words you habitually use. Start eliminating negative, hurtful words, and embrace positive, empowering words and watch your world change. You will enjoy a lot more Spanish mackerel!

12

On Technology

Ten Ideas on E-mail Etiquette

If you are old enough, you might remember ordering something from a catalog with the disclaimer *Allow 6-8 weeks for delivery*. When I told that to my grown children, they looked at me as though I had a third arm growing out of my head. Their response was "What?" When I go to the post office now, it feels strange, as if I have stepped into a time warp. E-mail is doing business at the speed of light. In order to be more effective, we need to remember a few things that haven't changed. This list is uncommon sense.

1) Check your spelling. Be aware of the TERRI-BLE TWO's TRAP: *too, two* and *to* all mean something very different, and they aren't the only homonym trap. Another is *there, their,* and *they're.* Last one, *than* and *then*: one compares value, the other has to do with time. Edit all your e-mails before sending. Know and use the correct meaning. The biggest sin is misspelling the other person's name. Look it up if you have any doubts. Better safe than sorry.

2) With e-mail, our knowledge of English (or lack thereof) is apparent to the world. Even though I write for a living, I am not an English snob. (Hey, I flunked tenth-grade English!) But come on! How many times have you seen misspelled words or poor grammar from people you respect? There are some basic skills each of us must master. If you are getting flack for your English, perhaps it's time to take a class or buy a good book on the basics. Load a dictionary app on your phone. When in doubt, check it out.

3) BTW, minimize the abbreviations, LOL!?!? It's okay in a text to your twelve-year-old daughter, but not to the CEO, or worse, a prospective client. It's just lazy; moreover, it will damage your credibility.

4) As long as we are on the topic, who was the inventor of emoticons (:-) and ;-) and :-0)? Again,

unless it's a really good friend, come on...not all the time with everyone. Moderation and common sense are the watchwords here.

5) Monitor your use of I, ME, and MINE. As with a face-to-face conversation, don't make it all about you. Count your "I to YOU" ratio in your last ten e-mails. Make certain your message is dominated by "YOU and YOURS" until it becomes a good habit. Be OTHER-Centered in your e-mails: "How is your family? Health? Bottom line? Sales?" Ask questions and listen like you would in person.

6) Your e-mail signature. Can a prospective client find you to contact you quickly and easily? At the very minimum, have your first and last name, e-mail address, cell phone, work phone, fax (yes, people still use faxes), Web site, and job title. Some people choose to have links to LinkedIn, Twitter, Facebook, a YouTube link (I have a five minute demo video in HD), and perhaps a quote or logo that summarizes your philosophy or your brand.

7) Your Subject Line is vital. Give some thought to what that says. It determines to a large extent whether your e-mail even gets opened. What action do you want your readers to take? What is the topic? Why is it relevant to them? Remember the six magic words: WHAT THAT MEANS TO THEM IS?

8) Only copy (cc) someone if he or she is part of the group and knows the other person. If you use bcc (blind carbon copy) let everyone know. People don't need to see all those names, but don't hide that fact either.

9) I love my brother. He is a very bright guy, an English teacher but, bless his heart, he writes three page missives in every e-mail he sends me, with no break in paragraphs. A new paragraph is a new thought or topic. Keep your e-mails short, to the point, and use separate paragraphs for separate thoughts and ideas.

10) Keep a journal or small notebook for written To-Do Lists just for important e-mail responses. Record action items and follow-up thoughts. Don't trust your memory. It's okay if you respond quickly to an important e-mail with your smart-phone, telling the person you will get back to him with more detail upon your return to your office. Remember to take an extra minute and jot it down. It will keep you from dropping the ball.

When evaluating retail service, what do you like as a customer? The same holds true for e-mail. What do YOU like? Do that with your clients, friends, prospects, and relatives. I have a good friend who always asks when he calls me, "Do you have a minute?" He means it. He is mindful of my busy schedule and he cares. What if you remembered that with e-mail? Don't send the "You'll love this" forwards from your Aunt Martha. How many kittens with monkeys do we want to see? Ask yourself, "Does this add value?" or "Will this be worth their time?" Empathy matters now more now than ever. We are all looking for ways to get TWICE AS MUCH DONE IN HALF THE TIME.

It really is true, we can have anything we want in life, if we only help enough other people get what they want first!

— Zig Ziglar, author,
speaker, philosopher

ACTIONS YOU ARE INSPIRED TO TAKE?

_____

_____

_____

_____

_____

_____

_____

_____

_____

_____

_____

It's About TIME

_____

_____

_____

_____

_____

_____

_____

_____

_____

_____

_____

_____

_____

_____

_____

_____

_____

_____

_____

_____

_____

13

ON KEEPING A JOURNAL

1982 was a turning point for me, a watershed moment in my life. The universe was conspiring to convince me to keep a journal. I was twenty-five years old, a technician in HVAC, working with Mike Alm, a gifted craftsman and a seasoned journeyman fitter/foreman. We were sitting in his truck waiting for the ferryboat from Bainbridge to Seattle. We had been remodeling a grocery store's refrigeration system for several weeks. He was writing in a notebook. "Do you have to keep an account of the job because you are the foreman?" I asked. He stopped writing, looked at me with the patient and kind eyes of a father, smiled and replied, "No. I want to get FROM the job, not just THROUGH it. That is what separates the good technicians from the great ones." I never forgot that.

The following spring, my wife and I went to Mexico for the first time (before kids). My mother had been a travel agent and always gave her repeat clients journals as gifts for the trips they were about to take. She gave me one for the trip. I took notes on the food we ate, the places we visited, and I pasted pictures into it. It was a twenty-minute-a-day investment. That was the best vacation I ever had. When a friend told me he was going to Puerto Vallarta, I was able to open my journal and make some great suggestions. He was grateful. I felt like Rick Steves. I was hooked on the value of keeping a journal. REAL MEN keep journals. I know, that's an in-your-face kind of statement, but it's true.

I have studied the lives of hundreds of great men and women. Who kept a journal? Here is a short list of great men who kept journals their entire lives...

- Teddy Roosevelt

- Thomas Jefferson

- Charles Darwin

- Thomas A. Edison

- Leonardo da Vinci

- Ben Franklin

- Andrew Carnegie

- Ralph Waldo Emerson

- Winston Churchill

- Sir Edmund Hillary

- Lewis and Clark

- Captain Cook

- Sir Ernest H. Shackleton

- John F. Kennedy

- Mohandas Gandhi

- Paul Allen

- J. Paul Getty

I could go on, but you get the idea. This is an impressive list indeed. The list of famous and successful *women* who kept journals is three times longer. Hmmm…

Clients and friends ask me almost every week, WHY do you keep a journal? Good question. Here is a subjective list, drawn from my own experience of over thirty years of journaling, of why I am committed to writing it all down:

For my children and my grandchildren, it's a kind of immortality, a written legacy.

It's a place for my goals and aspirations, my lessons learned, and for my WINS (anything positive worth remembering that feeds my soul and builds my self-respect and confidence).

My journal provides me perspective, distance from the initial challenge. After every presentation, be it a keynote to 1,500 people or a seminar to 50 people, that night before bed or on the airplane ride home, I answer two simple questions: "What went well that I want to repeat?" and "What can I improve for my next presentation?" This continuous improvement process began when I was new in sales 23 years ago. After every call, I would sit in my car and ask the two questions. By the end of my second year, my close rate was over 50 percent. Every book I read contains some new gem I capture in my journal. Get FROM the book, not just THROUGH it.

WHY ELSE?

- According to *The New England Journal of Medicine*, journal keepers visit the doctor half as much! Men keep things bottled up. Journaling lets the emotions out on paper.

- Journaling can bring you to your senses. Objectivity, perspective, and clear thinking occur when you write it all down.

- Journaling can pull you out of a depression. It can help you focus on what is really going on and assist in solving a tough challenge or setback.

- Journaling allows you to let go of the past, enjoy the present, and look forward to the future in a way nothing else can.

- Journaling can reduce your levels of stress. One Vietnam veteran attributes journaling to regaining his life and letting go of traumatic wartime experiences.

- Journaling can improve your relationships at home and work.

- Better organizational skills. A journal is a great place for your action items, to-do lists, and project notes.

- Improve your focus. It will expand your awareness, clarify challenges, and gain a new perspective on fuzzy thinking.

- "KNOW THYSELF." A journey of self-discovery allows you to see what brings you joy, what sets you off, who drags you down, and who pulls you forward.

- Journaling enhances your creativity and intuition; it's a place to mind-map ideas, projects, and values and goals.

- A journal is a place to catalog your journey, to remember the good stuff.

HOW do you keep a journal? It's easier than you think when you decide it's important to you. Here are some tips that will allow you to get FROM the day at odd moments:

- Carry a pen and notebook, 3 x 5 cards, or a journal with you at all times. When something strikes you, capture it.

- Write the date, time, location, day of the week at the top right-hand corner. This information will provide perspective when you re-read your journal. It will teach you WHEN and WHERE your best ideas come from.

- If you are a morning person, write in the morning. If an evening person, write at night. Surrender to when you are most productive and creative.

- WINS. When something positive happens in your life to you, your company, your children, or your spouse, write it down.

- When you have learned a painful or expensive lesson, capture it on paper.

- When a good idea interrupts you, write it down. Otherwise, chances are you will forget it an hour later. We have 60,000 thoughts a day.

- Capture vital information at work, critical conversations, quotes, notes, and bids. Jot them down.

- Short- and long-term goals, including to-do lists. Write down your six most important things to do today, along with how long you think they will take (e.g., thirty minutes) and then prioritize the list.

- Write just for yourself. Do not censor anything.

- Grammar and spelling don't count. <u>Misteaks</u> are okay.

- If you get stuck with writer's block, try answering a few questions: What was the most fun you had today? What have you been avoiding? Whom do you admire and why? What are five things you are grateful for? What one thing would you like to improve about your work? How can you be a better spouse or parent? Why did you close that last sale?

- Record, Inform, Organize, Reuse. When you consider these four elements, a journal takes on new meaning and value.

I fill up about four journals a year of all shapes and sizes. Some are lined, some are unlined. I have gigantic journals and tiny journals. The one I am using now is a six-by-twelve inch black leather journal. I carry it with me everywhere I go. I paste ticket stubs from movies and concerts, magazine and newspaper clippings, photographs, quotes, ideas, WINS, and lessons. Everything goes into my journal. I use a four-color pen. It separates thoughts and entries. When I want to TWEET or post on LinkedIn, I just open my journal and transcribe.

I need to find Mike Alm and thank him. He changed my life that day on the ferryboat. Now my kids keep a journal, as do many of my clients. They have told me that journaling changed their lives. Maybe it will change your life, too, and the lives of those future grandchildren. It will make you immortal. Now where is that pen? I have a great idea I want to capture…

P.S.

Many people are going digital with their journaling. Here's a list of desktop digital tools in which to keep your journal:

Word Processor. Simple and easy to use. Just open up MS Word or OpenOffice Writer and start writing down your thoughts and feelings.

why.OpenOffice.org

TextEditor/Notepad. Just open the text editor for your operating system, call the file "journal.txt," and start writing. Date each entry. If you're using Notepad, here's a nifty little hack that will automatically insert the date into your journal entry.

http://Lifehacker.com/185791/journaling-in-txt-with-notepad

JDarkroom. JDarkroom is a free Java-based text editor. What makes it different from other text editors is that it takes up the entire screen for distraction-free writing. It works on any platform.

www.CodeAlchemists.com/jdarkroom

OneNote. Microsoft OneNote is a cool note-taking program that can double as a journal. Just create a notebook within OneNote for your journal and start writing. You can easily drop photos and videos into your journal entries. OneNote is only available for Windows.

Evernote. Evernote is pretty much like Microsoft OneNote, except 1) it's free, 2) it works on any platform, and 3) you can save and access entries on the Internet easily, thus giving you access to your journal everywhere you go.

www.Evernote.com

The Internet provides several options for storing your journal in the "Cloud" and even share it with other people. A few options:

- Blogspot. It's free and it gives you the option of keeping your journal private or sharing it with a few people. In addition to writing text, you can easily include photos in your journal entries.

  www.Blogspot.com

- LiveJournal. This is pretty much the same as Blogspot. It's free and you have the option of keeping it private or you can share with others.

  www.LiveJournal.com

- WordPress. You can get a free wordpress.com blog and start a journal with it.

  www.WordPress.com

- Use Gmail as a journal. This is an interesting idea.

  http://Lifehacker.com/033239/gmail-as-a-journal

YOUR THOUGHTS ON JOURNALING

_____

_____

_____

_____

_____

_____

_____

_____

_____

_____

_____

_____

_____

_____

_____

_____

_____

_____

_____

The palest ink is better than the strongest memory. Get FROM the day, not just THROUGH it!

A journal is a kind of immortality. Long after you are gone, your grandchildren might just stumble across one of your journals and it could change their lives.

14

On Social Media

By the time you read this chapter, there is a good chance some of the information here about social media might have changed dramatically. That being said, here are some insights from my latest research into social media and its use in business. Social media is here to stay and growing geometrically every day.

For now, we will limit this discussion to the Big Three: LinkedIn, Twitter, and Facebook. Here are the best definitions I have found of their concept and benefits:

- **LinkedIn:** your CONNECTIONS, primarily business. Think of it as a giant Rolodex and Hoover's on steroids. [Hoover's Inc., a subsidiary of Dun & Bradstreet, is a business research company that provides information on companies and businesses.]

- **Twitter:** you have FOLLOWERS and are limited to 140 characters.

- **Facebook:** you have FRIENDS. Each one has a place in business.

Remember what Seth Godin said about posting anything online: "It's public and permanent graffiti that never goes away."

LinkedIn

If you are not LinkedIn, you will eventually be Linked-Out!

LinkedIn is the standard for online business networking. The average member is forty-three years old and makes $107,000 a year. It is the world's best networking database and growing every day. It's the perfect platform for helping people get what THEY want. It's gone from being a benefit to a necessity.

Sales have always been about Trust, Relationship/Likability/Competence/Value, and Timing. LinkedIn is like the old Rolodex on steroids, but with some very specific NEW RULES. The good news is, if you have ever had success in the past selling and marketing, you can leverage that knowledge, those skills, that attitude, and the habits/disciplines you need to succeed with LinkedIn. Nothing is ever lost. Everything counts.

As my friend Bob Burg says, "Become a Go-Giver! Go the extra mile with clients and friends. What can you give?"

My new friend, Kevin Knebl, says, "It's about delivering VALUE! Marketing means participating in activities that create opportunities to sell. Selling is what you get to do if your marketing works!"

HERE ARE SEVEN SIMPLE WAYS TO LEVERAGE LINKEDIN:

1) Update your profile. Let others know who you are, how to contact you, your experience, and credibility.

2) LinkedIn is your personal brand and personal/professional website. Just get started. You can always make the time later to update and improve your information.

3) Grab attention with a compelling headline, like "HOW TO GET TWICE AS MUCH DONE IN HALF THE TIME!" Then deliver.

4) Find out what the marketplace is looking for. Where is the pain? Offer solutions to that pain with your articles, special reports, e-books, books, CD/MP3s, DVDs, coaching, consulting, products, and services.

5) "Recommendations" reduce the risk for people considering doing business with you. Will Rogers said, "When someone else blows your horn, it travels twice as far." Gather quotes,

testimonials, kind words, and written praise. Don't be shy. "Unassertive salespeople and marketers have skinny kids."

6) Read a good book on social media. Kevin Knebl's *The Social Media Sales Revolution* will save you time and money. It will jump-start your commitment. It will demystify it all for you. It's a game changer. Buy it, read it, and do what he suggests. It's not as complicated and daunting as you think.

7) You don't go to the gym once a month and hope to get fit. Thirty to forty minutes a day, six days a week will get the job done with your wellness. LinkedIn is just like that. Twenty to thirty minutes is the length of the average sitcom. Turn off the TV and turn on LinkedIn. Learn something new every day for ninety days. You will become "socially fit" online!

Etch these wise words from Kevin Knebl into your brain:

- Remember, every connection that you have increases the value of your online network. *Never forget, at the end of the day, WHOM you know is more important than WHAT you know! You can never outrun your character. (Have character and avoid being one!)*

- In connecting with someone new, make certain you get the message across that you would like to create a mutually beneficial relationship, a win-win relationship.

- The creatures that have survived for millions of years were not the biggest. Just ask any dinosaur you see. Survivors are those that are the most adaptive. What worked five years ago doesn't work very well today. How will it be five years from now? The old sales phrase was ABC: "Always Be Closing!" That was great in the days of 8-tracks and rabbit ears on a black-and-white television set. Today, it's still ABC: although one word has changed: "Always Be Connecting!" online. LinkedIn accomplishes that with leverage.

- Your customers aren't spending much time on the phone these days...so why are you? If you want new customers, you have to go where they are—and that place is social media.

Kevin's book explains how to hunt down and sell to customers on all the major platforms. Learn how to change your focus from selling to marketing; expand your sphere of influence, become a value generator, and build your personal brand.

But hey, maybe you don't want to get twice as much done in half the time. That's okay. Just work fifteen hours a day and never see your kids or spouse. It's a simple choice—change or be left behind.

P.S.

Consider using TEMPLATES with LinkedIn to save time. Remember, "Connecting" is about offering VALUE! Here is one I have used in the past:

Great to hear back from you.

Life is so good. I am doing a great deal of traveling worldwide now (Canada, Istanbul, Australia). Working on my fourth book (self-publishing). By the way, if you would like to review that manuscript and offer up a quote for the inside cover, let me know. I would appreciate your opinion.

I attached a Special Report you might find useful. It's a kind of Mini-Seminar. Print, review with pen in hand, and look out. Your life might just change! What if you got twice as much done in half the time? Hey, that would be a great seminar (IT IS!).

Perhaps we can teleconference this month? What day and time is best for you?

Looking forward to catching up with you.

Mark

TWITTER

Twitter is proof that one great idea can change the world in weeks or months instead of years or decades. Consider its birth, overwhelming popularity, and use in its short existence.

Twitter is easy to set up. You are limited to 140 characters. I have mine set up with my LinkedIn page. When I post a 140-character comment on LinkedIn, it automatically sends it to my Twitter followers. It also appears on the home page of my Web site. Too cool and so simple.

Tweeting is about offering VALUE. Twitter is positive public graffiti. It's permanent. It's also a wonderful way to develop your online database and be exposed to great ideas, people, and insights. I only follow people I respect. It's geometric, organic, and exciting. In my second month of tweeting, I received an e-mail request for a seminar with an old client. THAT made my five-minutes-a-day commitment worth it!

Offer value and use good judgment. Never post anything negative or critical. Think of it as a front page headline in *The New York Times*. What would you want to see there? Once or twice a month, use a little shameless self-promotion and share an article you wrote, your website, an upcoming seminar, etc. Offer 80 percent value and 20 percent marketing and promotion. That is a good percentage to remember.

To create your own hash tag, just use the pound sign (#) and enter it as regular text with no spaces. Twitter will turn it into a link automatically when your tweet is posted. There is nothing else to it.

FACEBOOK

For the longest time, I resisted Facebook. It seemed like a waste of time. For 20 years I have been pretty ruthless with my time and with whom I spend it. So I procrastinated jumping into Facebook. I put it off for far longer than most other speakers I knew. I am self-employed; when I call in sick, I know I am lying. I made jokes about Facebook being for twenty-somethings and where old high school sweethearts reconnected. Then I came across this story:

Rodney Bradford, a 19-year-old man, would have never thought that a message typed on Facebook would become—literally—his passport to freedom. "Where's my pancakes," Rodney typed on Saturday, October 17, at 11:49 AM from his father's apartment in Harlem. The day after, the young man was arrested as a suspect in a robbery. His defense lawyer, Robert Reuland, used the Facebook entry, which was made at the time of the robbery, as his alibi. This was later checked by the district attorney, who dropped the charges as soon as the Facebook alibi was confirmed.

If you are reading this book, you probably don't need an alibi for robbery. That being said, it's difficult to ignore the following facts:

1. If Facebook were a country, it would be the third-largest country in the world. That's THIRD, after China and India, and BEFORE the good ol' USA.

2. Most people spend fifty-five minutes a day on Facebook EVERY day.

3. For some people, that is more time than they spend watching television.

4. There is a reason advertising dollars are flowing to Facebook. The reason is found in an old expression, "Go where the fish are." There are lots of fish in the Facebook pond.

5. Fifty percent of the most lucrative demographic, 18- to 34-year-olds, log onto Facebook as soon as they get up in the morning.

6. With 207,000,000 Internet users in the U.S., 71 percent of the American Web audience is on Facebook.

7. Forty-eight percent of Generation Y gets its news from Facebook.

8. Fifty-seven percent of people spend more time talking online than they do in person.

9. One out of thirteen people on earth is an active Facebook user and half of them are logged in on any given day.

Okay, so you are sold on creating a Facebook account and dipping your toe in the water. Are you afraid you will get too wet or drown? I feel your pain. Let us be clear about a few things: Facebook is not LinkedIn or Twitter; it's very different, so you must understand the protocol. Ninety-nine percent of the users are NOT there to buy something. They are there to talk with their friends and share pictures. Moreover, they DO NOT like to be sold. They are there to have a SOCIAL experience: to catch up with friends or family, meet new people, or share interests. It's like a twenty-year high school reunion 24/7/365.

Savvy users, of which I am not one, have two accounts. They have one for business and one for personal use. It's best not to mix business with your personal life.

We all have a comfort zone with disclosing personal information. Here are some questions to ask yourself before you commit to creating an account:

1. What is your goal for using Facebook?

2. How much time do you have for it each day?

3. Are you fluent with technology, or do you need your sixteen-year-old daughter to show you how to get started?

4. Is using Facebook going to help your business or improve your career?

5. Is it okay that it's just for fun?

Here are my answers to these questions:

1. I hope to use Facebook to drive people to my website, promote new books I have written, and find old friends from college and the military.

2. For me, 10 to 20 minutes is as much time as I am willing to commit, three times a week, or whenever the mood strikes me on my iPhone while waiting in line at the movies.

3. I need to hire someone to coach me (like my twenty-two-year-old son) to do it right.

4. I have low expectations about Facebook for now. As I research it, I am slowly changing my view.

5. Yes, it's okay. It IS fun.

Because of economies of scale, the geometric aspect of viral messages that only the Internet creates, and Facebook being perhaps the second-fastest spreader of ideas (after YouTube), here is another story that serves as a cautionary tale. It is a serious warning about keeping your word. We will call it, "THINK TWICE, TYPE ONCE":

A young Ecuadorian decided to open a group on Facebook under the name of "If I get 1,000,000, I, José Romero, will tattoo the 151 Pokemon on my back." He couldn't imagine the challenge would attract thousands of worldwide followers who were willing to support him in his exploit. Such was the euphoria of the people inspired by the boy's promise that 50,000 people had already joined the group after just 24 hours. He might have felt intimidated by the number of followers that grew by the second. He decided to suppress his profile so nobody could find him. The disappointed users of the group wanted to give him a drubbing for his prank and for breaking his word, so they created a Facebook page with an open call to find his whereabouts. The space has 600,000 followers so far!

If you develop a reputation for being dishonest or manipulative, you will quickly be ignored or derided on a mass scale. If you tell the truth, you don't have to remember what you said. Shakespeare wrote, "Oh what a tangled web we weave, when first we practice to deceive."

Earl Nightingale once said, "If honesty didn't exist, someone would most certainly invent it as the fastest way to become wealthy." J.C. Penney had it right when he founded his retail chain. He called his stores "The Golden Rule." In the world of Facebook, "Treat people the way you want to be treated" is good advice. Avoid sarcasm, witty put-downs, complaints, blaming, or negativity. Common sense and basic human relations skills apply.

Facebook *fan pages* are about promotion. On your fan page, there is nothing wrong with letting people know you have a product or service to provide. However, avoid going overboard. A non-stop sales pitch will turn people off. Post interesting information in which your fans see value.

As with Twitter and LinkedIn, VALUE is the watchword. 80 percent value and 20 percent marketing and promotion is a good mix. Keep in mind, all this information could be as anachronistic as 8-track tapes in a year. For now, I hope you have gathered a few nuggets to save you time.

Above all, remember this tenet: "Do not post anything you wouldn't want to see on the front page of *The New York Times*." Use good judgment, limit your time on Facebook, have fun, and remember to ask, "Where are my pancakes?"

ACTIONS YOU ARE INSPIRED TO TAKE:

_____

_____

_____

_____

_____

_____

_____

_____

_____

_____

_____

_____

_____

_____

_____

_____

_____

_____

_____

_____

_____

To Tweet or not to Tweet, that is the question.

Remember to offer VALUE. Online marketing is about providing ideas and information to improve and enhance the quality of other people's lives.

You will be the same person in five years but for two things: The PEOPLE you associate with (Twitter changes the game) and the e-BOOKS you read!

15

TEN WAYS TO IMPROVE LIFE AND WORK BALANCE

L ove the phrase, "What do you give someone who has it all?" Wouldn't it be nice if people were asking that about you? It's possible they could be if that is what you decide you want. Dial in a new thermostat setting and affirm it for thirty to sixty days. Here are some ideas that might assist you in achieving that end.

1. **Get Organized.** Clutter dramatically inhibits effectiveness. The feeling of worth and esteem attached to a neat, efficient desk, filing system, PC/Mac, closet, trunk, and life cannot be measured.

2. **Maximize Your Commute.** *Windshield University* will improve your K.A.S.H.: **K**nowledge, **A**ttitude, **S**kills, and **H**abits. Turn drive time into learning time. Learn a foreign language, brush up on your people skills, listen to an audio program on leadership, management, sales, or parenting. You get the idea.

3. **Exercise.** 30 to 45 minutes a day is all you need. Hey, that's two episodes of *Seinfeld.* I have lost 50 pounds and 10 inches from my waist in the last three years by making the time to get to the gym five days a week. Yoga, swimming, weights, stair-master, walking, basketball, spinning, or Zumba—pick one you like and are willing to commit to. Furthermore, a daily commitment for 90 days to portions (a meal is the size of your palm), quality (salad instead of fries), and exercise (walk daily) and you will drop 20 to 30 pounds from your frame. Simple, but not easy at first. The hardest part of a workout is GETTING TO THE GYM. My son, Colin, said to me recently when we were working out together, "Nothing tastes as good as skinny feels." Wow!

4. **Flexibility.** To retain talent, organizations are learning they must be flexible with their employees, i.e. flexible schedules and telecommuting. If you seek to become an "Employer of Choice" in your region, learn to be flexible with your associates.

5. **E-mail Vacations.** Take a break from being connected 24/7/365. "All work and no play makes Jack (and Jill) a dull boy (and girl)." Good advice. Hug your kids. Take the dog for a walk. The late business philosopher Jim Rohn said, "Wherever you are, be there!" Great advice.

6. **Leverage Technology.** This is the opposite of #5. Having your Droid or iPhone with you at your daughter's soccer game allows you to respond to the vital e-mails, but be aware of how much time your nose is in that device. Be strategic and limiting on how often you use it. Nothing beats seeing your child's face when she knows you saw her hit the winning goal!

7. **Walk Away.** Go for a walk. Disconnect. Take a dance class or yoga. Research tells us unless we disengage completely to refresh, renew, re-create, we run the risk of burning out, stressing out. Walking away is less about exercise than it is about disconnecting to gain some perspective. Detachment is the goal.

8. **Laugh It Off.** Humor, the healthy kind, bolsters your immune system and decreases stress. Read a joke book. Subscribe to a "Joke-of-the-Day" e-zine. Go to a comedy club or catch an improv skit. Find a way to laugh daily. I am fond of Jim Gaffigan, Rita Rudner, Steven Wright, George Carlin, Groucho Marx, John Pinette, and Louie Anderson.

9. **Keep a Journal.** I have been keeping my own journal since 1982. Log your WINS, write out your frustrations and challenges, capture a great quote, paraphrase a good story, or write out or mind map a goal. The palest ink is better than the strongest memory. Leave a legacy for your children and grandchildren.

10. **Plan Your Vacations.** Put them into your schedule and actually take them. We all need time away. One of the saddest things I hear is when someone brags that he hasn't had a vacation in five years. Two weeks in Hawaii, yes! A long weekend in San Francisco, yes! Some of my best ideas came while I was lying on the beach.

WHAT ACTIONS
WILL YOU TAKE FOR BALANCE?

_____

_____

_____

_____

_____

_____

_____

_____

You have to live on 24 hours of daily time. Out of that you have to spin wealth, pleasure, money, content, respect, and evolution of your immortal soul. Its right use, its most effective use, is a matter of the highest urgency...all depends on that.

— Arnold Bennett, author,
How to Live on 24 Hours

A final word: above all else, good time management is about event control and focusing on your highest priority items: first things first, one thing at a time, and finishing what you start. The past is gone and the future is only a concept, an idea with emotion. What is amazing to me is most people, 96 percent of the population, seldom grasp that self-evident truth; they don't GET THINGS DONE BECAUSE THEY DON'T HAVE THEIR GOALS WRITTEN DOWN! It really is a matter of time.

Efficiency is doing things right. Effectiveness is doing the right things. I learned a valuable lesson in my first year as an HVAC technician: If you lean your ladder against the wrong building, it doesn't matter how fast you go up and down it. It's the wrong building! Focus on becoming more effective. The juice is worth the squeeze.

Thomas Carlyle wrote: *Our main task is not to see what lies dimly perceived in the future, but to do the thing which lies immediately at hand.* John Ruskin had the word "TODAY" carved into a small marble block that he kept on his desk as a reminder to Do it Now! I have an hourglass as a reminder in my office. Remember, "YESTERDAY is a cancelled check, TOMORROW is a promissory note. TODAY is ready cash. Use it wisely!"

Make it an effective day. The best is yet to come!

YOUR NOTES

_____

_____

_____

_____

_____

_____

_____

_____

_____

_____

_____

_____

_____

_____

_____

_____

_____

_____

_____

_____

16

ON GRATITUDE

My mother used to say, "If you have your health, you have everything." I used to think that was so cliché. Not anymore.

This is a true story about Josephine, a woman in her late fifties, who was diagnosed with a malignant brain tumor. While waiting for the operation, she sat on her porch swing and gave thanks for all the wonderful things in her life. She wrote a letter of thanks to each of her family members. The night before surgery, she had a dream, a vision so real it changed her. In it, a woman came to her and, as Josephine described it, said, "'Everything is going to be okay.' She assured me I would have plenty of time to fulfill my life's purpose. 'Always remember that it is your

love and appreciation that brought this healing to you.'"
The next day, the doctors were astonished. The tumor
was gone.

Stories like that, though unbelievable to some, are
commonplace. The science of psychoneuroimmunology,
introduced to a wider audience by Norman Cousins in
the 1980s through his bestselling book *Anatomy of An Illness*, proves to us that gratitude affects our health.

The Norman Cousins Center for Psychoneuroimmunology at UCLA investigates the interactions between the
brain and the body, the role of psychological well-being
for health and recovery from illness, and the translation
of such knowledge into effective behavioral strategies that
prevent disease, promote healing, and enhance well-being across a lifespan.

Positive emotions strengthen our immune system,
which enables us to resist disease and recover more
quickly from illness. Gratitude, optimism, and laughter
all serve to release endorphins into the bloodstream.
Endorphins are the body's natural painkillers that stimu-
late dilation of the blood vessels, which leads to a relaxed
heart. Conversely, negative emotions such as worry, anger,
resentment, fear, self-pity, and hopelessness slow down
the movement of disease-fighting white cells in our bloodstream and contribute to the development of stroke and
heart disease by dumping high levels of adrenaline into
the bloodstream.

In other words, FEAR kills. FAITH heals. We all need *Freedom From Fear* (the title of my first book, available from www.SparkingSuccess.net).

I am a true believer. Why? Five years ago, I was at death's door. Three days after my surgery in 2007 (I had a foot of my colon removed), I was not processing food. I was rushed back to the hospital a second time and the doctors removed my appendix and more of my colon. I should have died twice. During my recovery, I read up on this science of healing. I made it a point to give thanks every day, aloud and on paper. I also made it a point to laugh every day. Moreover, I am on a mission to make other people laugh every day as well. Laugh, Love, Learn, Leverage, and Leave a Legacy. Those five L's represent my life's purpose. I have made the time every day since 2007 to live those five L's, my L-5.

You cannot be grateful and unhappy at the same time.

Melody Beattie wrote, *Gratitude unlocks the fullness of life. It turns what we have into enough, and more. It turns denial into acceptance, chaos into order, and confusion to clarity...Gratitude makes sense of our past, brings peace for today, and creates a vision for tomorrow.*

There are certain laws that operate whether or not we are aware of them. They are timeless laws, immutable principles that just are. Gratitude is one of those mysterious laws. The more gratitude we have, the more abundance we receive. The more cynical and ungrateful, the less we get.

By becoming grateful, we set in motion a kind of magnet, attracting people, emotions, and attitudes that foster abundance. I don't completely understand it, but hey, I don't understand why my wife likes cut flowers. I buy them; they eventually die and are thrown away. However, I understand the effect. "Oh!" she exclaims. So I keep buying them. Gratitude is like that.

When you combine gratitude with a positive expectancy, something magic happens; you become an "Inverse Paranoid": someone who feels strongly that the world is out to do him good! Great things just start happening. Great people show up in your life. Great days become the norm. So how do I foster an "Attitude of Gratitude"?

Begin by making a "Gratitude List." What are Ten Things (or People) for which (whom) you are grateful? Make your list now:

1. _____

_____

2. _____

_____

3. _____

_____

4. _____

_____

5. _____

_____

6. _____

_____

7. _____

_____

8. _____

_____

9. _____

_____

10. _____

_____

When you find yourself having a tough day, grab a pen and paper and make a list. What makes you smile? What is great about your life right now? You see, it's impossible to be in the light and the darkness at the same time. They cannot coexist. When you focus on what you are grateful for, pessimism, cynicism, and negative attitudes disappear. You are transformed. I have made hundreds of these lists over the last thirty years. They truly are magical.

Optimism will sneak up on you in the process. Guess what? Optimists live longer than pessimists. Moreover, they have a better time along the way.

It's a choice, *A Simple Choice* (the title of my third book available at www.SparkingSuccess.net).

Consider these quotes from great thinkers of the twentieth century:

Celebrate what you want to see more of.

— Tom Peters

We can only be said to be alive in those moments when our hearts are conscious of our treasures.

— Thornton Wilder

As we express our gratitude, we must never forget that the highest appreciation is not to utter words, but to live by them.

— John F. Kennedy

At times our own light goes out and is rekindled by a spark from another person. Each of us has cause to think with deep gratitude of those who have lighted the flame within us.

— Albert Schweitzer

Be thankful for what you have; you'll end up having more. If you concentrate on what you don't have, you will never, ever have enough.

— Oprah Winfrey

He is a wise man who does not grieve for the things which he has not, but rejoices for those which he has.

— Epictetus

Let us be grateful to people who make us happy; they are the charming gardeners who make our souls blossom.

— Marcel Proust

WHO ARE THE FIVE MOST GRATEFUL AND POSITIVE PEOPLE YOU KNOW?

1. _____

_____

2. _____

_____

3. _____

_____

4. _____

_____

5. _____

_____

How can you spend more time with them?

Did you know that how you feel affects your personal and professional productivity?

You have control over your thoughts, emotions, and attitudes. Where is your focus?

What if you got into the habit of being grateful? When someone asks how you are, simply say: "I am so grateful to be on this side of the grass. Life is so good." The pessimists will flee. The optimists will smile, agree with you, and offer good news from their lives. It's simple. It's the Law of Attraction. Birds of a feather really do flock together.

Who are you attracting? It all starts with an Attitude of Gratitude!

17

ANYWAY!

I read a little book entitled *Anyway* by Kent M. Keith. He lists the 10 Paradoxical Commandments. They remind me of my youngest son, Evan. In December of 2010, my wife and I flew to Oahu to watch Evan play basketball, three games on three islands. His team won all three, and it was a defining moment in his college basketball career. After I read *Anyway*, it hit me—Evan lives many of these commandments. Here are a few...

If you do good, people will accuse you of selfish ulterior motives. Do good ANYWAY!

If you are successful, you will win false friends and true enemies. Succeed ANYWAY!

The good you do today will be forgotten tomorrow. Do good ANYWAY!

Honesty and frankness make you vulnerable. Be honest and frank ANYWAY!

I encourage you to pick up a copy of *Anyway* and give it a read. I think you'll find it as profound as I do.

Robert Alm is a successful attorney and banker who lives in Hawaii. He created a program called the Live Aloha Program. The meaning for *Aloha* that the program had in mind deals with caring, affection, and courtesy. Here is the list of its examples:

- Respect your elders and children

- Leave places better than you found them

- Hold the door for others

- Hold the elevator for others

- Plan something

- Return your shopping cart

- Get out and enjoy nature

- Pick up litter

- Share with your neighbors

- Create smiles

Simple ideas. What if you tried them out for thirty days, even if people think you are strange? Try them ANYWAY.

Evan's coaches, friends, teammates, and teammates' parents tell me with great regularity how nice our son is... all 6' 11" of him. That doesn't mean he isn't a competitor and doesn't want to win. He blocks your shot, and then helps you up! I think it's because he lives those Ten Commandments. He got them from his mother!

As of this writing, Evan has been invited to a tryout with the NBA team, The Golden State Warriors in October of 2012. All his hard work has paid off. He has a terrific foundation of labor, focused effort, discipline, and goal achievement. He will go as far as he sets his mind to. ANYWAY, that's enough from the proud Dad.

18

ON MENTORS

I have a long list of mentors to thank for the person I have become. My first mentor, when I was fourteen, was Bob Moawad. He changed my view of what was possible. In that life-changing "Action for Excellence" seminar in 1973, I took fifty pages of notes. I set written goals for basketball and achieved them. I set written goals for school and went from a 1.8 GPA to a 3.8 GPA. I learned how to visualize. I learned many of the things I have written about in this book. Bob Moawad was a gifted teacher, coach, and motivator.

He was at once charismatic, funny, insightful, caring, and smart. Moreover, he was the coach I wished I had. Eventually, I went to work for him. Those four years changed my life forever. I applied the time-management ideas he taught and GOT TWICE AS MUCH DONE IN HALF THE TIME. He made it easy for me to approach men I respected and ask them for help.

Charlie "Tremendous" Jones was another man who transformed the way I saw the world. He saw something in me. He believed in me. He said, after reading the manuscript for *Freedom From Fear*, "If you can write another book like that, you won't need to speak anymore!" Whoa! Few people ever affected me in such a profound and meaningful way. He and Bob had many things in common. They were both:

- Enthusiastic

- Positive

- Driven

- Caring

- Focused

- Outgoing

- Smart

- Life-Long Learners

- Focused on Family and Balance

- Great Speakers

- Terrific Marketers

- Super-Salesmen

- Optimistic

- Funny

- Leaders in Their Field

Susan Hall was my German teacher in high school. She was an extraordinary educator. Had she taught math, I would have been an accountant. She was directly responsible for getting me into the business of speaking. She convinced me to come back to my old high school and give a talk. That led to another talk, which in turn led to another. I realized this business of speaking was not only fun, it was something I was good at. I began reading everything I could find about public speaking. In 1990, I stumbled onto an article in *Contracting Business Magazine* about Harvey Mackay, the famous author of *How to Swim with the Sharks Without Being Eaten Alive.* The article was a revelation to me. I read it 50 times. It set me on a path for the next 22 years. I am now living the life I read about in that article. Thanks, Susan!

In 2007, I was speaking to 500 contractors in Yuma, Arizona. I invited Susan Hall to attend. In my PowerPoint slides, I created one slide that read: "Five Great Things I Got from Susan Hall." I had her stand up. The crowd gave her a standing ovation.

You might never have an occasion to do something like that, but you can write that teacher, coach, boss, uncle, or aunt a letter or an email. Speak from the heart. Tell your mentor how he or she positively impacted your life. Here are some thought-provoking starter questions to get your juices flowing:

WHO are the people who have had the biggest impact on your life?

_____

_____

_____

_____

WHY were they so inspiring to you?

_____

_____

_____

_____

WHAT did they bring out in you?

_____

_____

_____

_____

WHERE are they now?

_____

_____

_____

HOW can you reach out to them? (LinkedIn, Google, e-mail, letter)

_____

_____

_____

_____

WHEN will you write that letter?

_____

_____

_____

_____

WHAT will you tell them?

_____

_____

_____

_____

Send that letter. It will make a profound difference in your life and theirs. Do it today. Don't wait. Life is short. You just never know whether you will run out of time to thank that person for making a difference in your life.

19

TEN COMMANDMENTS FOR MANAGERS

I have been on this spinning, big blue orb for 55 years now. That is time enough to have learned a few things. I consider myself a pretty smart guy; however, I am constantly amazed by how stupid I was two years ago—and the cycle repeats. Yet, every once in a while, I hear or read something that takes me aback and I simply must write it down. Here it is: "You must learn to place less value on all that you can remember and more on those few things that you must never forget." Marcus Buckingham wrote that in his terrific 2005 book, *The One Thing*

You Need to Know: About Great Managing, Great Leading, and Sustained Individual Success.

In my first 30 years, I had a lot of horrible bosses and a few really great ones. The very best managers stood out. They were ruthless managers of their time, yet they were kind and tactful. They were assertive and never wasted a minute, yet made you feel important. They got talked about. We all knew who they were. We might not have agreed with what they said or did, or understood why they did what they did, but we liked how they made us feel. I had the extreme honor of being hired by some really great managers and leaders. I paid attention. I watched what they did and said. I listened to the language they used with others and with themselves. I wrote it all down.

Do you remember the Billy Crystal movie *City Slickers?* Jack Palance's pitch-perfect character, Curly, was the grizzled, stone-faced loner and ranch trail boss, a real cowboy. He stole every scene he was in. Billy's character was Mitch Robbins, a clueless city slicker trying to build rapport and engage Curly in conversation, but without much luck. Finally, Curly told Mitch, "The secret [of success] in life is just one thing." Curious, Mitch asked, "What is that?" Smiling as he rolled another cigarette, Curly replied, "That's your job to find out what that one thing is." Mine was writing and speaking. It took me 32 years to figure it out. In the 1987 album *The Joshua Tree*, U2 vocalist Bono lamented, "I still haven't found what I'm looking for." Most of us haven't.

A manager is not the same thing as a leader. Managers manage people. It's one-to-one. A manager grows people. He inspires change, coaches up, teaches specific skills, and encourages people to take risks and stretch comfort zones. He brings out the best in people. He truly cares about those he serves. It really is true: You can have everything you want in life if you only first help enough other people get what they want or need.

Here is my list of 10 Disciplines/10 Principles/10 Commandments to master. They represent the things we must never forget if we are managers. It might not be a complete list, but it's a great start. Think of them as ten goals to master over the next five years.

1. **Fall in Love With Your Work (Organization and Industry)**

   Great managers love their job. They are proud of the company they work for. They are hardworking and loyal. They take 100 percent responsibility for their actions and decisions. They are at once coaches, teachers, and servant leaders who teach by able example. Great managers smile a lot. They seem to genuinely love what they do and wouldn't dream of doing anything else. Their attitude is contagious. They talk about their work away from the job. They love talking with other managers in their industry and are always looking for, and finding, new and better ways of getting things done. If you do what you love, you'll never work another day in your life.

2. **Become a Lifelong Student**

   Great managers read books and trade magazines. The books you don't read won't help.

They attend every seminar they can. They are sponges for any information that will help them reach their goals. Great managers pick the brains of other people who are more successful. They find mentors. They keep a journal to capture lessons and ideas, and they borrow boldly from the best. They practice the "Hour of Power": 20 minutes Reading, 20 minutes Planning, and 20 minutes Thinking and Affirming their goals every morning (or evening) without fail.

3. **Get Great At Sales (and Marketing)**

Everyone is in sales. The only question is, "How good are you at it?" Selling is both a science and an art. The science is in the math. What is your close ratio? Out of ten prospective deals, how many do you close? Do you close 10 percent, 20 percent, or 50 percent? You need to know. That is how you track your progress and skill. You are either green and growing or ripe and rotting. There is no neutral in business. The art is the people side of the equation. We make buying decisions based on emotion and justify them with logic. Selling is like a chair with four legs: Trust, Relationships, Competence, and Timing. People buy from people they like, trust, and believe. How good are you at asking great open-ended questions and actively listening? As a manager, you are selling all day long. You sell internal customers (associates) on the company values, ideology, and vision. You sell external customers who give you the chance to demonstrate your competency. We are all in sales. How good are you at it?

4. Know Thyself (and Others)

What is the best and highest use of your time and talent? One secret of successful managers is they know and understand their gifts and strengths. At the same time, they are brutally honest about their shortcomings and weaknesses. They invest most of their time in the things they are good at and delegate those tasks that are their weaknesses. They solicit feedback from technology (MMPI, DISC, personality profiles, etc.), the people they serve, and the people they report to. They are flexible, willing, and able to change. They are change masters. They have thick skin and cold blood. They are serious about improving and pay the price in advance.

5. Set Big Hairy Audacious Goals (and Lots of Little Ones, Too!)

Great managers set BIG Goals like "Increase sales by 30 percent this year while maintaining a gross profit of 40 percent!" They have crystal-clear expectations of each job and employee. They create clear job descriptions and walk through each bullet point with each associate. "What do you get paid to do?" is a vital question! If you ask a receptionist, she might say, "I get paid to answer the phone." "No," you say in a kind, soft tone, "you get paid to solve clients' problems by telephone and do whatever it takes to delight them." Focus on WHAT you want and WHY! Leave the HOW up to the employees. First we work on goals and then they work on us. Be absolutely clear on your expectations of yourself and others. Peter Drucker asked, "What is your contribution to the organization?"

6. **Track and Measure Everything**

As a sales manager, your goals need to be made clear by publicly posting both the goals and activity, month by month, in a public place. For example, everyone needs to know: "Mark Matteson sold $75,000 and is 300 percent of sales plan!" How many service agreements were sold? What about projects? How many did you lose last year? The term "churn" is the percentage of clients who left measured against the total. Less than five percent is great, but more than 10 percent is bad! Where performance is measured, performance improves. What are you measuring?

7. **Reward Behavior You Want Repeated (the Window and the Mirror)**

Whatever gets rewarded gets repeated. Whatever gets punished stops. That is the greatest management principle in the world. What do you want to see more of? What do you want to see less of? Praise pays. High-fives in the hallway, ringing of the bell, awards, trophies, plaques, and cold hard cash given in public settings, like annual meetings or monthly meetings, matter to the people you manage. You are making a statement. Get creative and make the acknowledgment public. Reward the Sales Star of the Month with movie coupons, gift cards, or paid time off. Remember the Window and the Mirror: When it comes time to take credit for the success, look out the window and give it away—to your team! When it comes time to assess blame, look in the mirror and assume full responsibility. What gets rewarded gets repeated.

8. **Hire Hard, Train Easy**

This discipline is easier said than done. What is your ratio of interviews to hires? Is it 2:1, 5:1, 10:1, or 20:1? The larger the first number, the lower the turnover and the higher the productivity. Great managers understand and accept this; poor managers are lazy with this commandment. Who do you allow on the bus? Are they in the right seat on the bus? This is huge when building your team. My friend, Chuck, was a master of this. He was great at developing relationships with the right people. He was patient, persistent, and relentless in pursuing and hiring great people. He built a $25 million dollar commercial HVAC service company in twenty years from $800,000 in 1980. He trained liked crazy. When the CEO was lamenting the overall cost of training new people, Chuck said "There is only one thing worse than training someone and then having them leave. That is if we don't train them and they stay!" Hire up. Hire young Turks who want your job. Talent deprecation is hiring down. They in turn hire down, and that person is serving your customer. If you are a "six", hire an "eight"; they will hire "tens"!

9. Become a GOOD-Finder

Are you a GOOD-Finder or a FAULT-Finder? What if you got in the habit of praising people in public? The very best managers I have seen are great at acknowledgement and recognition. "Treat people as they are, they remain. Treat them as they can be, they become." Catch people in the act of doing things right. This is simple, but not easy. It's a habit. Each of us moves toward pleasure and away from pain. My publisher used to say, "You know what I like about you? EVERYTHING!" Research and the successful organizations around the globe have proven one thing: Employees who are cared about produce more, stay longer, and are easier to get along with. Care more than others think is wise. Become a GOOD-Finder. Praise pays.

10. You Have a Team of People

In a bacon-and-egg breakfast, the chicken was INVOLVED, but the pig was COMMITTED! Do you want compliance or commitment? Get your team involved in the ideation process. Break them into groups to brainstorm and ask the right questions: "How can we generate more leads from the field?" and "What will inspire you to action (time off, cash, movie tickets)?" As the coach goes, so goes the team. Keep searching for new ideas. Master the previous nine disciplines. The answers will come. Invest in education for both you and your greatest asset, your people. Education always brings a return, not once, but many times over. Ben Franklin said, "Take a coin from your purse and put it in your head. It will come flowing from your head and overflow your purse." Ben understood.

These are the things we must never forget and remember to do.

One last thing: have fun. Life is short. The best is yet to come. The secret to life is just one thing. That's your job. Find out what that one thing is. Thank Curly. Giddy up!

20

A FINAL WORD

If you made it this far, perhaps you are willing to go a little further. To get the most from this book, here are some ideas to assist you in GETTING TWICE AS MUCH DONE IN HALF THE TIME.

1) Repetition is the mother of skill. Review your notes and the portions of this book you under-lined, highlighted, and annotated. Your notes are always the most important part of the process of learning.

2) Read this book again with a pen or highlighter in hand (in case you didn't the first time!).

Think of this book as a guide, a compass, a tool to help you go from HERE to THERE!

3) Keep it with you and refer to it often.

4) Rewrite your goals onto 3 x 5 cards and carry them with you. Put them where you will see them daily: on the fridge, on the mirror where you shave or apply your makeup each morning, and on the dashboard of your car. When you have a spare moment, waiting in line at the bank or getting gas, or stuck in traffic, say your goals aloud and think about how wonderful this future state will be and what it will mean to you to achieve it. Capture the feelings of positive expectation.

5) List the REASONS you want that goal. What will it mean to you? REASONS pull us to the future. It opens up our R.A.S. (Reticular Activating System). It's the HOW function of the brain.

6) Follow your hunches: Read that article, pick up that book, e-mail that person, or call that friend. I have earned so much business over the last 25 years by listening to the still, small voice, my hunches. Emerson called it the "Iron String." Napoleon Hill called it "Infinite Intelligence." Some people call it "A God Shot." Whatever it is, it has our best interests at heart. Listen to it. Follow it. It's one of the answers to your goal question.

7) Find Five Mentors. A mentor is someone who has done what you want to do and been where you want to go. Develop a relationship with your five mentors. Some of them offer training, coaching, consulting, seminars. Invest the time and money. At the very least, ask them to lunch and pick up the tab. Bring your journal and ask them five questions:

   a) What books should I be reading?

   b) What seminars should I be attending?

   c) What would you do differently if you were just starting out?

   d) Whom can you introduce me to that you feel I should get to know?

   e) What else?

8) Read every book you can find on the goal you are reaching for. Start with the books and e-books your mentors suggest, and then read five more. Become an expert on your goal.

9) Write everything you learn in your journal. Capture the ideas, quotes, questions, answers, action items, insights, and go back over them on a regular basis. Get from the day, not just through it.

10) Share what you have been learning with someone else on a similar path. It's called "Dual Plane Learning." In order to teach it, you have to learn it thoroughly. It's also good karma.

By helping someone else, you are helping yourself. It's the Law of the Harvest, reaping and sowing; it's cause and effect. What if you shared this book with five people you care about? How much better would you feel? Invest in giving to others on a regular basis; it will change your life. Buy copies and give them to others; or e-mail the e-book with a note, "I hope you get half as much from this book as I did."

Last, but not least, one final life-changing idea: What kind of legacy will you leave? I have one letter from my father. I have a couple of dozen pictures and my memories, both positive and negative. That's it. What if you wrote a letter to your great-grandkids telling them all the things you hoped they needed to know to be successful in life and business?

The late, great Steve Jobs spoke at Stanford in 2011, just before he died. Here is what he said:

Remembering (on occasion) that you are going to die is the best way I know to avoid the trap of thinking you have something to lose. You are already naked. There is no reason not to follow your heart. Things don't have to change the world to be important. The only way to be satisfied is to do what you believe is great work. It's only by saying NO that you can concentrate on the things that are really important. Don't let the noise of others drown out your inner voice. Stay hungry. Stay foolish.

Life is short. Make the most of yours. Remember to enjoy the journey; the best is yet to come. Thank you for investing in yourself. Will Rogers wrote, *A man only learns in two ways: one by reading and the other by association with smarter people.* If you follow that advice, it's not IF you will reach your goals, but WHEN!

James Allen wrote over one hundred years ago, *Circumstance does not make the man, it reveals him to himself. Men do not attract that which they want, but that which they are. Not what he idly wishes and prays for does a man get, but what he justly earns. His wishes and prayers are only gratified and answered when they harmonize with his thoughts and actions.*

Persistence and a constancy of purpose is what is needed to achieve tremendous and seemingly impossible long term goals. In Clint Eastwood's extraordinary film, *Invictus,* we learn that Nelson Mandela (played pitch-perfect by Morgan Freeman) read the William Ernest Henley's poem *Invictus,* from which the film took its name, every day in his prison cell for 27 years. It served as a kind of compass for him pointing him to his own True North. Maybe it will do the same for you. Mr. Mandela changed the world. He did more than just hope and pray. He developed relationships with his guards. He learned their language, customs, and passions (rugby). Only after the work did the results come. Some say ending Apartheid was a miracle. Perhaps. I like to believe it was his faith in timeless principles, and his application of those ideas in daily life, that changed the world.

INVICTUS

Out of the night that covers me,
Black as the pit from pole to pole,
I thank whatever gods may be,
For my unconquerable soul.

In the fell clutch of circumstance,
I have not winced nor cried aloud.
Under the bludgeonings of chance,
My head is bloody, but unbowed.

Beyond this place of wrath & tears,
Looms but the horror of the shade,
And yet the menace of the years,
Finds, and shall find me, unafraid.

It matters not how strait the gate,
How charged with punishments the scroll,
I am the master of my fate;
I am the captain of my soul.

Steve Jobs said, "Go make a dent in the universe."
It's About TIME, isn't it?

About the Author

Mark Matteson started his career as an HVAC technician in 1976. He is one of those rare professionals who can say he is a speaker, consultant, and author and *mean* it. He has attracted clients in HVAC contracting, distribution, and manufacturing as well as such high-profile organizations as Microsoft, T-Mobile, John Deere, ConocoPhillips, Aflac, and over 100 Fortune 1,000 companies on three continents. He typically conducts 40 Keynotes, 20 Seminars and Workshops, and 5 to 10 Consulting engagements annually around the world.

A committed writer, Mark has written five books including the international bestseller, *Freedom from Fear* that has been translated into Japanese and French. Mark is also the author of popular e-books including *Presenting Like a Pro, Sales Success Strategies,* and *Customer Service Excellence.* His monthly e-newsletter goes out to 6,000 people a month since 2003. He tweets and comments on LinkedIn daily.

Mark is interviewed frequently and has been quoted in the media. He is considered a thought leader, an idea reporter, and agent of change who teaches his clients HOW TO GET TWICE AS MUCH DONE IN HALF THE TIME. He has worked in 47 states and internationally in Australia, Canada, Aruba, and Turkey.

Mark resides in Edmonds, Washington with his wife of 34 years, Debbie.

Mark takes great pride in the fact he once flunked high school English.

CONTACT
INFORMATION

To book Mark to speak to your company, association, or conference, call or e-mail:

Phone: 206.697.0454

E-mail: Mark@SparkingSuccess.net

To watch his inspiring demo video, visit:
http://SparkingSuccess.net

To subscribe to Mark's monthly FREE e-newsletter, go to www.SparkingSuccess.net and fill in the required boxes.